LIFE AT THE TOP

NEW YORK'S MOST EXCEPTIONAL
APARTMENT BUILDINGS

LIFE AT THE TOP

NEW YORK'S MOST EXCEPTIONAL
APARTMENT BUILDINGS

KIRK HENCKELS
AND ANNE WALKER

PHOTOGRAPHY BY
MICHEL ARNAUD

VENDOME

NEW YORK · LONDON

CONTENTS

INTRODUCTION

F ASCINATION WITH REAL ESTATE IS NOT A NEW PHENOMENON, AND NEW YORK CITY'S rich and varied array of luxury apartment buildings has long held particular allure. From the moment the stately and picturesque Dakota arose on the undeveloped land of the Upper West Side in the early 1880s, the city's great apartment houses, with their elegant façades and distinctive silhouettes punctuating the skyline, their sprawling floor plans and exquisitely designed interiors, have never ceased to intrigue. Because of Manhattan's limited geography and rapid population growth at the end of the nineteenth century, expansion was possible only northward and upward. These dictates—combined with the invention of the elevator— contributed to the creation of the apartment building as we know it. What began with the Dakota as a novelty has become a building type that New Yorkers can truly call their own.

Life at the Top is an account of New York's most splendid apartment buildings over the past 130 years, from Henry Hardenbergh's Dakota (1884) to Rafael Viñoly's 432 Park Avenue (2015). In essence, the book traces the development of apartment living for the top echelons of New York society through two major transitions. The first began at the end of the Gilded Age, when a growing number of wealthy New Yorkers migrated from fussily ornate Belle Époque mansions into elegantly designed apartment buildings. The second began at the turn of the twenty-first century with Richard Meier's sleekly contemporary Perry Street towers and continues to this day. Both transitions were fueled by remarkably similar factors: a wave of staggering wealth accumulation, the development of new technologies and materials, a desire for a more convenient, less cluttered "modern" lifestyle, a need to build vertically, and an increasing focus on major architects, now known as "starchitects," and exceptional interior designers.

Before 1900, the concept of apartment living had emerged but remained the precinct of the lower and middle classes; the townhouse was still considered the norm. As *The Architectural Record* remarked in 1901, "To the New Yorker of thirty years ago, the apartment house was an exotic. Every good Knickerbocker, with even the most modest pretensions, considered it his duty to house his family with four walls wherein he would be the sole lord and master; and the highest reach of his ambition was a

New custom grillwork in a living room at River House, inspired by architect William Lawrence Bottomley's original grillwork in the lobby of the building, covers the addition of air-conditioning vents. A gilt French opera chair sits in front of the window. The silk curtains are embellished with a hand-embroidered thistle pattern.

brownstone front."[1] Gradually, however, the economies and conveniences of vertical living expanded to the higher economic and social echelons, culminating in the widely publicized construction of the Dakota on Central Park West. Though the Dakota may have been built for people of means, it was not intended for the top tiers of society. It remains a virtuosic exemplar of late nineteenth-century architecture and layouts: a stylistic confection, labeled variously as German Renaissance and Gothic Revival, featuring an elegant carriage entrance accessing an interior courtyard and expansive rooms with high ceilings and sumptuous finishes. For its time, the Dakota offered state-of-the-art services and technology, including a private dining room for residents, hydraulic elevators, and electric lights.

The definitive moment for Manhattan's luxury apartment living arrived in 1912 with McKim, Mead & White's 998 Fifth Avenue, located directly across from the Metropolitan Museum. It was palatial and without peer. Each of the seventeen enormous apartments was appointed with the finest of details, including high, coffered ceilings, imported paneling, elaborate plasterwork and moldings, and a long, spacious gallery. As the American champions of the Beaux-Arts tradition, McKim, Mead & White designed 998 in the refined neo-Italian Renaissance style that dominated the ensuing building boom of equally grand, elegant apartment houses along Fifth and Park Avenues on the Upper East Side. The all-limestone building also provided a large staff of porters and elevator operators, thereby reducing the number of servants needed by the individual owners. Nevertheless, each apartment had five or six small servants' bedrooms, a "servant's hall" for staff meals, secondary back staircases, laundry and pressing rooms, and locked rooms for valuables. The building became so renowned that it was referred to simply as "998" or as "The Millionaires' Apartments." The latter name was particularly appropriate, as it was the first apartment building on the stretch of Fifth Avenue known as "Millionaire's Row," a series of single-family mansions that at one point were home to half of the millionaires in the United States. Although 998 was designed for the wealthiest New Yorkers, it faced the challenge of being accepted by high society. Despite the increasing costs of maintaining a Manhattan mansion and the imposition of federal income tax in 1913, New York's most affluent continued to look askance at apartment living. As legend has it, James T. Lee, 998's developer, offered Senator Elihu Root a discounted rate to sign a lease, which effectively broke the social taboo on multifamily residences. It wasn't long before 998's occupants included a Vanderbilt heir along with Winthrops, Guggenheims, and a former vice president.

The success of 998 triggered the first boom in opulent apartment house construction, which lasted through the 1920s and early 1930s but was brought to an abrupt end by the Depression. The period saw the predominance of a classical style, far more refined and elegant than the previous Victorian and Edwardian styles, as well as the emergence of the streamlined Art Deco style in the late 1920s. Fortunately, this era was blessed with truly gifted architects, including J. E. R. Carpenter, Rosario Candela, and Cross & Cross. The original owners of apartments in these buildings lavished attention on their interiors, decorating the walls with art, often installing imported architectural details to enhance their living space, and commissioning the services of talented interior designers. They and succeeding generations of residents looked to designers like Dorothy Draper, who created many of Manhattan's most remarkable apartment lobbies, Elsie de Wolfe, Jean-Michel Frank, and Sister Parish. Today, the most renowned designers of the age vie for the opportunity to decorate an apartment at 740 Park, the Beresford, or any other of the fifteen buildings featured in this volume.

The majority of these elegant structures are on Fifth and Park Avenues, though at least three were built along the banks of the East River before the construction of the FDR Drive prevented their occupants from yachting to Wall Street. Astors, Phippses, Morgans, Rockefellers, and members of almost every other prominent New York family moved into these buildings. Remarkably, these exclusive prewar cooperatives with their strict social and financial admittance requirements continued to dominate Manhattan's luxury housing market for more than eighty years.

"He's not ours. Try River House."

The rarified world of New York's luxury apartment buildings and the multifaceted functions of the doormen—the keepers of the gates—have been subject to the wit of *New Yorker* cartoonists for years.

Arguably, no buildings with truly large, grand apartments were built between the 1930s and the advent of the twenty-first century. At the turn of this century, however, a new round of massive wealth accumulation instigated the most radical change in luxury housing preferences in a hundred years. Just as 998 Fifth heralded the transition to a classical style and grand apartment buildings on the Upper East Side, the tremendous success of the Robert A. M. Stern–designed 15 Central Park West in 2005 signaled a clear shift toward high-rise apartment buildings, contemporary styling, and a renewed emphasis on building services. The forty-three-story condominium includes such amenities as a private driveway to screen residents from paparazzi, a screening room, and a professionally equipped, 14,000-square-foot fitness center with a 75-foot swimming pool. This trend has coincided with the rejuvenation of lower Manhattan neighborhoods such as Tribeca, the High Line in Chelsea, the Financial District, and the Flatiron that previously had been as remote to the city's upper echelons as the Dakota in the 1880s. This is evidenced by the large number of new construction projects designed by such "starchitects" as Richard Meier, Norman Foster, Zaha Hadid, and Herzog & de Meuron. Nonetheless, the grandest and most costly of these new, exceptionally tall towers are located in Midtown. The finest example of this trend is 432 Park Avenue at 56th Street, designed by Rafael Viñoly. At 96 stories, it is currently the tallest residential building in the Western Hemisphere—at least until the next one is completed—and appeals to the significant influx of hugely wealthy foreign buyers.

This book chronicles the dramatic shifts in lifestyle and design that have marked Manhattan's most luxurious residences over the past 130 years. From Beaux-Arts mansions to predominantly classically styled cooperatives and then, eighty years later, to high-rise glass condominiums. From downtown to uptown and back downtown again. From formal, seated black-tie dinners for forty with forty in staff to order-in meals from the building's gourmet restaurant. Such transitions always generate intense debates between the various factions: uptown versus downtown, classical versus contemporary. Regardless of one's stylistic preference, there is still truth in the expression *de gustibus non disputandum est*, or "in matters of taste, there can be no dispute."

THE DAKOTA

IT WAS THE DAKOTA, THAT STAUNCHLY PICTURESQUE APARTMENT HOUSE ON CENTRAL PARK West, that signaled the beginning of luxury apartment living in New York. Built by Singer Manufacturing Company tycoon Edward C. Clark in the early 1880s, it was constructed at a time when the Upper West Side was a relative no-man's-land: remote, inaccessible, and undeveloped. When completed in 1884, the Dakota occupied one of the highest points in the city—the West Side plateau. As its surroundings were entirely open, the apartments had expansive views of the entire island, from the Hudson to the East River, and the building was visible for all New Yorkers traveling up and down Manhattan. "Probably not one stranger out of fifty who ride over the elevated roads or on either of the rivers does not ask the same of the stately building which stands west of Central Park, between seventy-second and seventy-third streets," the *Daily Graphic* proclaimed.[1] Indeed, the Dakota represented something entirely new, especially in an area still rife with shanties and barren, unleveled fields. The Ninth Avenue (now Columbus Avenue) elevated railway, established in 1879, connected the Upper West Side to lower Manhattan, and the new American Museum of Natural History had opened on Central Park West in 1877, but still the area was slow to develop because of its challenging and rocky topography. But, its pioneering location notwithstanding, the Dakota was remarkable: "the largest, most substantial and most conveniently arranged apartment house of the sort in the country."[2]

At a time when small apartment buildings were just debuting, the Dakota's developer, Edward Clark (1811–1882), was something of a visionary. A classically trained lawyer, he became associated with Isaac Merritt Singer, a rough-around-the-edges inventor who was seeking legal advice. With a keen business sense, Clark parlayed this connection into half ownership of Singer's firm, the Singer Manufacturing Company, and built the business up to such a degree that Singer sewing machines became a household name. Clark accumulated a fortune and in the mid-1870s began to diversify his interests. Focusing on New York real estate, he bought a number of blocks in the West 50s, 70s, and 80s in the hope that "a new era in building [was] about to commence, in which intelligent combined effort will produce novel and splendid results." He felt that the West Side "should be built so as to accommodate a great number of families, some

OPPOSITE *Wood Ducks*, 1880, by Arthur Nahl hangs above a Kimbel and Cabus ebonized cabinet decorated with Minton tiles and ceramics by Christopher Dresser.

ABOVE When the Dakota was finished in 1884, the Upper West Side was still undeveloped. Its completion initiated the first wave of apartment building on Central Park West.

RIGHT Actress Lauren Bacall was a resident of the Dakota for more than fifty years.

splendidly, many elegantly, and all comfortably. That the architecture should be ornate, solid and permanent."[3] On his travels abroad, Clark had observed how Europeans lived, and he began developing, in rapid succession, small apartment buildings modeled on French flats, including the Van Corlear (1879) on Seventh Avenue between 55th and 56th Streets and the Wyoming (1880) on the southeast corner of Seventh Avenue and 55th Street. Also in 1879, he built a small apartment house and twenty-four rowhouses on West 73rd Street between Columbus and Amsterdam Avenues. For all of his building ventures he turned to Henry Janeway Hardenbergh (1847–1918), an emerging architect who in 1876 had designed a folly on Oswego Lake near Cooperstown, New York, for him. The great-great-grandson of the founder of Rutgers College, Hardenbergh had apprenticed with Detlef Lienau, a German-born architect educated in the Beaux-Arts tradition. Hardenbergh's association with Clark was opportune, coming at a moment when the city was rapidly expanding and New Yorkers were changing the way they lived. He went on to design the Plaza Hotel in the same German Renaissance style in 1907.

As the story goes, the building's location—so far north and so far west—inspired its name, but Clark also tapped into the Indian territories for the names of some of his other developments, including the Wyoming and the Ontiora (1882) on the southwest corner of Seventh Avenue and 55th Street. The Dakota singlehandedly instigated the development of the Upper West Side and gave Manhattan's upper-middle class a luxurious and comfortable model for apartment living on a par with what might be expected from a brownstone. When it was completed—two years after Clark's death—the sturdy, square, fortress-like buff-colored brick edifice trimmed in Nova Scotia stone was unlike anything the

LEFT John Lennon, arguably the Dakota's most famous resident, leans against the ornamental railing on the roof, February 24, 1975.

BELOW Nina Bernstein and her brother, Alexander, in the apartment of their father, Leonard Bernstein, January 1, 1984.

city had seen. Indeed, the Dakota was solid and elegant, but Hardenbergh's profusion of bays, niches, balconies, cresting, finials, turrets, oriels, and terra-cotta ornament infused the ten-story building with a fairy-tale element—a massive château, complete with a dry moat. The two-story mansard roof, originally reserved for servants' quarters, was the building's most prominent feature, sporting picturesque gables, peaks, copper details, and layers of dormers peeking out of its steep pitch. An elegantly arched carriage entrance with high iron gates and a groin-vaulted ceiling gave access to the inner sanctum: an interior courtyard resembling one that might have been found in Paris. Hardenbergh lavished attention on the finer things: wrought-iron railings in the shape of double dragons and bearded characters, carved images of Indians, the Singers, and creatures of the imagination.

The building was well planned and modern. Hardenbergh located four small lobbies clad in marble wainscoting with Mexican onyx trim and intricate ironwork details at the four corners of the courtyard,

which accessed the elevators and bronze stairs. Thanks to the courtyard, all of the building's sixty-five suites were well lit and ventilated, and the apartments, ranging from four to twenty rooms, provided accommodations for everyone from bachelors to large families. With expansive rooms, fourteen-foot-high ceilings, private halls, and sumptuous finishes, including bronze mantels, tiled hearths, intricately carved wood details, and mahogany and oak wainscoting, the interiors were exceptionally lavish and grand. The conveniences, including electric lights and modern kitchens and bathrooms, were unparalleled at the time. In keeping with modern apartment design, Hardenbergh positioned the larger public rooms facing the street and the kitchens facing the interior.

As an enclave on the undeveloped Upper West Side, the Dakota was a world unto itself. A first-floor private dining room for residents, catered by the building's kitchens, resembled a baronial hall in England with its inlaid marble floors, English quartersawn oak paneling, bronze relief work, and massive carved-brownstone fireplace. The basement, lit by skylights in the courtyard garden, included a barbershop, a kitchen and pantry, bakeshops, workrooms, and a laundry. On the tenth floor, space was reserved for a children's playroom and gym. Later, residents could enjoy the Dakota's garden, a private croquet lawn, and a tennis court built on the roof of the underground boiler house, located behind the building between 72nd and 73rd Streets. A staff of 150 ensured that the building ran smoothly and efficiently. In September 1884—one month before its designated opening—25 percent of the apartments had been leased, with rents ranging from $1,000 to $5,600 per year. By the 1890s, there was a waiting list.

Throughout its history, the Dakota has continued to intrigue and draw interest. In the 1880s and 1890s, a host of successful professionals—stockbrokers, lawyers, merchants, professors, and doctors—rented apartments. Perhaps some of the best known were music publisher Gustav Schirmer; educator John A. Browning, founder of the Browning School; and Frederick G. Bourne, the Clark family agent and future president of the Singer Manufacturing Company. After the Clark family turned over the ownership of the Dakota and it became a cooperative in the early 1960s, a great number of creative and artistic types moved in, giving the somewhat tired building a glamorous renaissance. It became a magnet for celebrities, including Lauren Bacall, who lived there for fifty-three years, Judy Garland, Ruth Ford, Lillian Gish, Jack Palance, and Robert Ryan. In the 1970s, composer Leonard Bernstein, film critic Rex Reed, and designer Ward Bennett moved in. Russian-born dancer and choreographer Rudolf Nureyev occupied a six-room pied-à-terre—one of his seven homes—in the 1980s and 1990s, dramatically decorated with giant allegorical paintings and colorful wallcoverings. Roman Polanski's 1968 psychological thriller *Rosemary's Baby* cast the Dakota in a more sinister light, the building's dark, brooding exterior the stage for the cult film, which starred a young Mia Farrow running through dark hallways and cavernous rooms. John Lennon, the building's most famous resident, purchased an apartment on the seventh floor in 1973. He and his wife, Yoko Ono, went on to purchase several more suites in the ensuing years. Lennon's 1980 assassination at the entrance of the building brought the Dakota to the world's attention as waves of mourners came to grieve at the base of the grand edifice—the exact spot where the former Beatle had been gunned down.

Although the Dakota was originally built for the city's aspiring upper-middle class, rather than for its social and business elite, it stands today as one of Manhattan's best buildings, still attracting a broad spectrum of artistic types and business leaders. With laser-sharp acuity, Edward Clark accomplished what he set out to do in 1880, creating a building that was not only solid and permanent but also architecturally splendid.

BEDROOM
18' × 11'

BEDROOM
20' × 12'6"

CL

CL

BEDROOM
20' × 16'

CL

CL

LIBRARY
18'6" × 16'6"

LIVING ROOM
18'6" × 29'

GALLERY
13' × 16'

CL

BEDROOM
13' × 20'

CL

CL

VESTIBULE

CL

WIC

CL

MAID'S
ROOM
8'6" × 6'6"

PANTRY
8' × 11'

DINING ROOM
18'6" × 24'

STORAGE

CL

CL

CL

MAID'S ROOM
9'6" × 9'6"

KITCHEN
12' × 19'

AMERICAN ARTS AND CRAFTS

With its high ceilings, expansive rooms, and beautiful woodwork, this apartment represents the very best of the Dakota. As just its third owners in its 130-year history, Deedee and Barrie Wigmore have only enhanced the beauty of its well-preserved nineteenth-century bones with period décor and artwork. The American Aesthetic movement, which flourished in the 1880s, championed art for art's sake and celebrated color, pattern, and ornament in the service of both sensory delight and utility. As collectors, the Wigmores acquired appropriate furnishings by the likes of Herter Brothers and Kimbel and Cabus and incorporated wallcoverings and marquetry typical of the Aesthetic style throughout the apartment. Also emblematic of the late nineteenth century, a series of well-lit Hudson River School paintings accent the apartment's long hallways and capacious wall space. Something of a time capsule, this apartment authentically captures the essence of what it might have been like to live in the Dakota at the time it was built. A visual treat, it abounds in artistic interest and brings back the world of the Dakota of yesteryear. . . . but with the latest conveniences of the twenty-first century.

The foyer features an Aesthetic-style sofa, a companion to one in Chateau-sur-Mer, one of the first Gilded Age mansions in Newport, Rhode Island. Above it hangs *End of an October Day*, 1880, by Walter Launt Palmer. An elephant-shaped majolica jardinière sits on a library table by Kimbel and Cabus. *The Woods in Autumn*, 1878, by Sanford R. Gifford hangs on the opposite wall.

ABOVE An American brass-and-cloisonné chandelier hangs in the foyer.

RIGHT An Aesthetic movement mirror over the library table in the foyer is seen through the portière.

OVERLEAF The furnishings in the living room include a center table by Frank Furness, a Philadelphia-based architect, and a side table by Herter Brothers. Nineteenth-century American paintings grace the walls, including *Woodland Interior* by John F. Kensett over the Herter table on the left; *Low Tide, Grand Manan Island* by Alfred Thompson Bricher to the left of the fireplace; and *Lake of the Clouds, Mount Mansfield, Vermont* by Edmund Darch Lewis on the wall to the right. P. B. Wight's Lily wallpaper was supplied by Bradbury & Bradbury.

OPPOSITE Among the furnishings in the library are a drop-front desk by Kimbel and Cabus, a garden stool by Christopher Dresser, and an ebonized table, also by Kimbel and Cabus, topped by a brass lamp. Jervis McEntee's *Mist Rising near New Paltz* hangs above.

ABOVE In the library, a ceramic plaque depicting an exotic bird, decorated by Ernest Carrière for Théodore Deck pottery, hangs above a bookcase designed by Frank Furness. Ceramics by Christopher Dresser and Burmantofts adorn the top.

BELOW Another ceramic plaque by Carrière for Théodore Deck, entitled *Duck in Flight*, hangs above four 1880s vases from Rookwood Pottery, Cincinnati, Ohio.

OVERLEAF The ebonized dining room table was commissioned by Judge Henry Hilton; his house was featured in the nineteenth-century publication *Artistic Houses*. Paintings include (from left to right) *Conway Meadows, New Hampshire,* 1869, by Albert Bierstadt; *Rushes, Easton Pond, Newport, Rhode Island,* 1877, by William Trost Richards; and *Harvest Moon, Giverny* by Charles H. Davis.

LEFT The dining room features
several different wallpaper
patterns. The walls are covered
with Oxborough Trellis from J.
R. Burrows & Company; Birds
Swooping is used for the frieze
and Raindrop for the ceiling
cove, both from Bradbury
& Bradbury. The ceiling
is decorated with Cracked
Ice, a custom paper from
Scalamandré.

OPPOSITE BOTTOM
Herter Brothers designed
the two sideboards in the
dining room. *No Man's Land,
off Martha's Vineyard*, 1878, by
Sanford R. Gifford hangs above
the sideboard in the foreground.
Walter Crane designed the
screen over the far sideboard; it
was executed by London's Royal
School of Art Needlework in
1876. A circular faience plaque
of two magpies by Théodore
Deck decorates the hallway off
the dining room.

RIGHT An upholstered chair
by Herter Brothers and a brass
and silver-plate table by W. T.
Mersereau & Co. sit beneath
Charles H. Davis's *Harvest
Moon, Giverny*.

LEFT Because the apartment has had only three owners in its history, all of the woodwork details are original, including a whimsical gargoyle carved in the ash mantel.

BELOW The master bedroom includes a suite of ebonized furniture by Herter Brothers. An oval ceramic plaque by William S. Coleman hangs above the mantel.

RIGHT Seen from a bathroom with tiled walls and an encaustic tile floor is a bedroom furnished with a Herter Brothers bed and a bedside table by A. & H. Lejambre, Philadelphia. *The Student*, 1884, by Walter Launt Palmer hangs above the bed.

BELOW Above the bedroom's elaborately carved wood mantel is a ceramic charger by William S. Coleman.

ABOVE *Windsor From the Thames* by Andrew Melrose hangs above the mantel in the kitchen. Decorating the mantel is an Eastlake clock with Japanesque tiles by Palmer, Bachelder & Co., Boston, and French vases attributed to Baccarat. Ceramic chargers by William de Morgan and a corner cabinet by Kimbel and Cabus enhance the hallway to the laundry room.

OPPOSITE The kitchen features the apartment's original cabinets and a Kimbel and Cabus table. The patterned encaustic tile floor and the various wallpapers create visual interest.

· 998 ·
FIFTH AVENUE

I N 1909 REAL ESTATE DEVELOPER JAMES T. LEE (1877–1968)—BEST KNOWN AS THE GRANDFA-ther of the late Jacqueline Kennedy Onassis—embarked on the first upscale apartment building on Fifth Avenue, or "Millionaire's Row," as it was known—a groundbreaking effort at a time when private houses were still considered the norm for the city's rich. In the early 1900s, the stretch of the avenue along Central Park consisted primarily of large Victorian townhouses, Beaux-Arts mansions, and veritable châteaux designed by the likes of society archi-tects C. P. H. Gilbert and Richard Morris Hunt. Indeed, the whole Upper East Side was a low-rise neighborhood with just a few tall buildings. Despite the success of some of the early apartment buildings on the West Side, multiple dwellings were still thought of as the precincts of the lower and middle classes. Up to this point, Lee—who had graduated from Columbia Law School—had developed one apartment building: the comfortable, mid-level Peter Stuyvesant on 98th Street and Riverside Drive. His notion of creating an apartment building with interiors comparable to those of the houses along Fifth Avenue was revolutionary and signaled the beginning of a shift from private houses to mansions in the sky that would continue to gain momentum over the next decade.

Operating as the Century Holding Corporation, Lee and his partner, Charles R. Fleischman, purchased a lot on the northeast corner of 81st Street, opposite the newly expanded Metropolitan Museum of Art, from financier August Belmont Jr., also the founder and chairman of the Interborough Rapid Transit Company. Belmont had intended to build his own mansion on the site but instead remained in his house on 34th Street until he later relocated to an apartment in the newly completed 820 Fifth Avenue. For 998 Fifth Avenue, Lee enlisted McKim, Mead & White

OPPOSITE In the Guggenheim apartment, the entertaining rooms were laid out in an enfilade. In the living room, an arched doorway embellished with French boiserie sits on axis with the variegated marble mantelpiece in the adjoining dining room.

to design a twelve-story limestone Italian Renaissance palazzo. The firm was considered the best of the best, even after the recent deaths of its two most prominent partners, Charles F. McKim and Stanford White. In the 1880s and 1890s the firm had been instrumental in introducing the Italian Renaissance style to New York City as a means to express the importance and cultural awareness of its newly "arrived" inhabitants. Clubs, such as University and Metropolitan, and private houses, such as the Villard Houses at Madison Avenue and 51st Street, were

ABOVE The twelve-story Italian Renaissance–style limestone building designed by McKim, Mead & White was the first luxury apartment house on Fifth Avenue.

BELOW LEFT Executed in a pinkish cream Botticino marble, the lobby was one of the building's selling points. Several steps led up from the entrance vestibule to the lobby's main hallway, where elevators, lined in French walnut, accessed the apartments above.

BELOW RIGHT A grand marquise signaled the otherwise understated side-street entrance on 81st Street.

modeled on Italian palazzos—a measure that instilled a certain gravitas, street presence, and aura of rootedness and dignity. In this vein, McKim, Mead & White designed 998 Fifth Avenue as a great, oversize palazzo with reserved, tasteful ornament and an impressive denticulated cornice. The building's limestone façades, heavy rusticated base, quoins, and string courses and reliefs at the fourth, eighth, and twelfth floors gave an impression of solidity and permanence.

As described by *Architecture and Building* magazine, 998 Fifth was a "suitable structure to its location and its apartments are designed for the residential use of those who could afford to own Fifth Avenue residences and maintain them."[1] It offered every convenience of a private house while eliminating many of the disadvantages, including the need for an extensive staff. Built on an essentially square footprint, it was constructed around a terra-cotta-lined interior courtyard, designed to increase the reflection of light, and contained seventeen apartments: one duplex maisonette, two full-floor apartments, and the remainder—the typical arrangement throughout most of the building—two simplexes and one duplex every two floors. McKim, Mead & White detailed every inch of space in their plans, ensuring that all of the interiors were carried out with an elegant touch. A mix of Georgian and Tudor finishes, extensive paneling, and a range of marble mantelpieces, as well as up-to-date heating, ventilation, and vacuum systems promised that the new accommodations would be both luxurious and comfortable. Lavish but dignified, the lobby and hallways were executed in a pinkish cream Botticino marble, and the elevators, lined in an exquisitely grained French walnut, featured elaborate ironwork; a grand marquise signaled the otherwise understated side-street entrance. All of the simplex apartments contained a long gallery modeled after the gallery at Haddon Hall in England, complete with a geometrically patterned strapwork ceiling reminiscent of the original and windows overlooking the courtyard. It connected the public rooms, which looked out on the park, including the Adam-style dining room, the living room, and an ellipse-shaped salon ornamented with delicate plasterwork. All of the duplexes faced 81st Street and the rear of the building.

As the building was underway, apartments began to rent. Senator Elihu Root, who had commissioned an elegant Carrère & Hastings townhouse on the corner of Park Avenue and 71st Street just six years earlier, signed on as the first tenant, reportedly paying nearly $25,000 a year for a full-floor apartment on the tenth floor. A member of New York's elite, the Nobel Prize–winning statesman was just the person to galvanize others of his ilk to lease apartments. His occupancy at 998 Fifth was highly publicized and soon others followed suit, including Levi Morton, former governor of New

York and the twenty-second vice president of the United States under Benjamin Harrison; Mrs. Elliott Shepard, daughter of William H. Vanderbilt; Goldman Sachs partners Ludwig Dreyfuss and Henry Goldman; mining magnate Murry Guggenheim; and Watson Bradley Dickerman, former president of the New York Stock Exchange. Col. George B. Fearing and Henry Rogers Winthrop, presidents of the Knickerbocker and Piping Rock Clubs, respectively, furthered the acceptance of apartment living among the city's bluebloods.

As an article in the *New York Times* put it in 1913, "The house has no name. It does not need one. It is called by its number. And it is so famous that even the name of the avenue is not added. It is always spoken of, among the elect, as '998' and nothing more."[2] Today, 998 stands much as it did back then: a quiet, dignified palazzo with one of New York's best addresses that has attracted some of the city's most influential and affluent denizens and foreigners for more than a century.

ABOVE LEFT W. B. Dickerman's living room doubled as a gallery; its walls were covered in fabric and hung with an impressive collection of paintings.

ABOVE RIGHT Antiques dealer Édouard Jonas's library was decorated with Vincent Van Gogh's *Portrait of a Peasant* and Edgar Degas's *Dancers in the Wings* and *Horse with Head Lowered*.

LEFT McKim, Mead & White designed the simplex apartments with a long gallery modeled after the one at Haddon Hall in England, featuring geometrically patterned strapwork on the ceiling and wood-paneled walls.

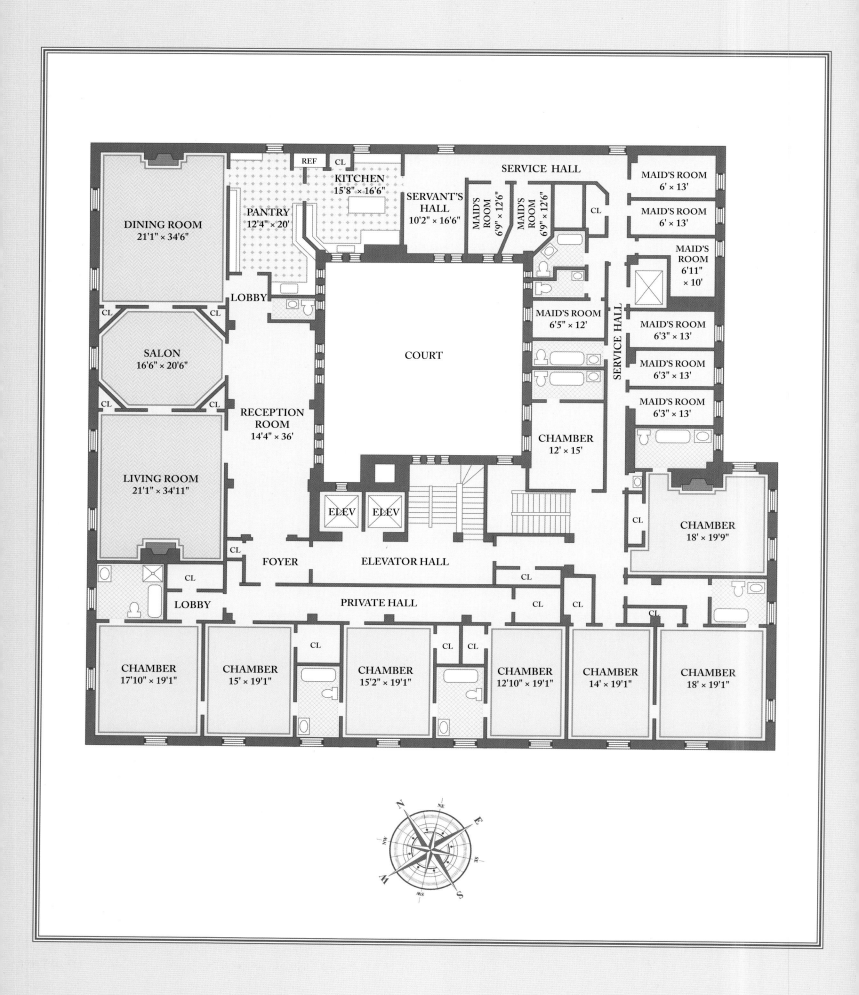

DINING ROOM
21'1" × 34'6"

REF

CL

KITCHEN
15'8" × 16'6"

SERVANT'S
HALL
10'2" × 16'6"

SERVICE HALL

MAID'S ROOM
6' × 13'

MAID'S ROOM
6' × 13'

PANTRY
12'4" × 20'

MAID'S
ROOM
6'9" × 12'6"

MAID'S
ROOM
6'9" × 12'6"

CL

MAID'S
ROOM
6'11"
× 10'

LOBBY

SALON
16'6" × 20'6"

CL

CL

MAID'S ROOM
6'5" × 12'

MAID'S ROOM
6'3" × 13'

SERVICE HALL

COURT

MAID'S ROOM
6'3" × 13'

RECEPTION
ROOM
14'4" × 36'

CL

CL

MAID'S ROOM
6'3" × 13'

LIVING ROOM
21'1" × 34'11"

CHAMBER
12' × 15'

ELEV

ELEV

CHAMBER
18' × 19'9"

CL

CL

FOYER

ELEVATOR HALL

LOBBY

CL

PRIVATE HALL

CL

CL

CL

CL

CHAMBER
17'10" × 19'1"

CHAMBER
15' × 19'1"

CL

CHAMBER
15'2" × 19'1"

CL

CL

CHAMBER
12'10" × 19'1"

CHAMBER
14' × 19'1"

CHAMBER
18' × 19'1"

BEAUX-ARTS LEGACY

Expressly designed for mining magnate Murry Guggenheim and his wife, Leonie, this apartment featured a series of custom-designed rooms and special elements, including gold-plated hardware produced by Tiffany & Co., special light fixtures, and elaborate French boiserie. The 1913 *New York Times* article proclaimed the twenty-five-room suite, with a rent of $25,000 a year, to be the "world's costliest apartment."[3] Instead of going ahead with the standard McKim, Mead & White design for the space, the Guggenheims commissioned the design firm of L. Alavoine & Company, popular for its French interiors and Regency paneling in some of Newport's most celebrated mansions, to inject the rooms with a decidedly French flair. In the long gallery, the Guggenheims opted for a ceiling of translucent glass and sinuous ironwork ornamentation that cast softly radiant light. In more recent years, Thomas Jayne has updated the historic interiors with comfortable yet appropriate furnishings. His color schemes highlight the architecture of the rooms, while a series of French and American works on paper—a departure from the old masters and Impressionist paintings one might expect—give the apartment a more youthful and lighter feel. The incredible ironwork and intricate carvings—representative of turn-of-the-century taste—have been maintained and showcased in the design, as have other more utilitarian details such as the original call-button panels and the silver safe in the kitchen.

OPPOSITE Floor plan. One of the building's two full-floor apartments. The public rooms stretch along Fifth Avenue and the bedrooms along 81st Street. The extensive servants' quarters are to the rear.

BELOW LEFT The rusticated four-story stone base supports the floors above; to enliven the façades, the architects incorporated carved reliefs between windows, a balustrade above the fourth floor, and pediments above the openings on the fifth floor.

BELOW RIGHT String courses at the fourth, eighth, and twelfth floors divide the façade into sections, and quoining at the corners of the building give it a solid street presence.

LEFT The gallery features marble Ionic columns and a ceiling of translucent glass overlaid with wrought-iron detailing.

ABOVE The front door in the entrance hall is embellished with ironwork and gilding.

OVERLEAF Colorful prints from *Jazz* by Henri Matisse contrast with the elaborate woodwork and moldings in the music room. Thomas Jayne designed the cocktail table after a Maison Jansen model once in the collection of the Duke and Duchess of Windsor.

PAGES 46–47 The living room, anchored by an early twentieth-century Indian carpet, is furnished with an array of upholstered sofas, chairs, benches, and a suite of fauteuils by the famous French eighteenth-century cabinetmaker Georges Jacob.

TOP The music room includes an original roundel painted with a depiction of Euterpe, the muse of music.

ABOVE The living room features delicate boiserie above the windows.

OPPOSITE Thomas Jayne painted the walls of the living room a shade of blue with a strié finish to enhance the original architectural details of the space.

OVERLEAF An aubergine-and-pistachio-hued Persian rug informs the color scheme of the dining room. The walls are painted green with a strié finish. Their marbleized bases were executed by Pierre Finkelstein.

LEFT A window in the library overlooks Central Park.

BELOW The wood-paneled library was originally a billiards room.

OPPOSITE TOP The master bedroom features a molded niche for the bed.

OPPOSITE BOTTOM Ferguson & Shamamian Architects transformed a former bedroom into a media room. A lithograph by Jasper Johns has pride of place on the wall.

LEFT In the garden room, Pierre Finklelstein's trompe l'oeil painting gives the space architectural character. Eighteenth-century chairs surround a round table with a gray marble top. An eighteenth-century bust of a woman by François-Marie Poncet looks on. The owners had a pair of tables made with metal bases that are covered with lichen moss. One of the tables can be seen on the far left.

BELOW Basil Walter designed the garden room in the Italianate style to match the style of the building.

GILDED AGE MAISONETTE

This apartment has been a continuing work in progress since its owners acquired it twenty years ago, after it had undergone an extensive modernization in the 1970s. Working with architect Basil Walter of BWArchitects, they sought to restore the apartment to its former glory, using McKim, Mead & White's original drawings, now housed at the New-York Historical Society. By restoring old details and reinstating others that had been lost, they re-created the original architecture of the apartment. They also redesigned the kitchen and bathrooms with history in mind. The kitchen incorporates period cabinets, materials, and even appliances, and the bathrooms include original tubs, showers, and fixtures that they painstakingly tracked down. In the garden—a slice of land once occupied by one of the street's original brownstones, which was demolished in 1931—they replaced a modern Japanese-style addition with a more appropriate garden room in the Italianate style of the building. Starting with virtually nothing to fill the apartment, the owners have gradually accumulated a substantial and beautiful collection of antiques, furnishings, sculpture, and artwork that suits the grand proportions and historic ambience of McKim, Mead & White's rooms. Along the way they've benefited from Thomas Jayne's expertise in historic décor, Gina Bianco's unerring eye for textiles and much more, and the masterly work of Pierre Finkelstein's Grand Illusion Decorative Painting.

ABOVE The owners found McKim, Mead & White's original front hall covered in thirty coats of red paint when they moved in. Now, articulated plaster walls by Finkelstein simulate the effect of stone and set off the original architectural details. The owners decorated the space with an eighteenth-century marble-topped, gilded-wood French table, an eighteenth-century mirror, and a Greek cuirass.

OVERLEAF The suite of Louis XVI furniture in the living room was upholstered by restoration upholsterer Diane Welebit. Above the sofa hangs a portrait of the Bourbon del Monte family by Francesco Podesti, ca. 1829. An eighteenth-century Aubusson carpet anchors the space. Though the antique Viennese chandelier has been electrified, it can still burn candles.

LEFT The blue damask wallcovering and the upholstery on the chairs flanking the fireplace were made by Renaissance Textiles using old looms and old dyes. The seventeenth-century Isfahan rug was from Hubert de Givenchy's collection.

BELOW The woodwork in the library had been dyed red; Pierre Finkelstein restored it to its original color, matching the room's original doors, which were still in place. The original mantelpiece is flanked by small sixteenth-century Italian and Flemish paintings.

An eighteenth-century
French tapestry hangs above
a sofa flanked by two George
II walnut library chairs
upholstered in fabric from
Humphries.

LEFT The dining room's original paneling and mantelpiece create a dignified backdrop for the antique English dining table, William Gomm chairs, ca. 1763, and the English Regency ormolu-and-glass chandelier.

ABOVE An eighteenth-century French urn rests atop a cipollino marble pedestal.

TOP AND RIGHT Using McKim, Mead & White's drawings as a guide, the owners re-created a semblance of the original kitchen. The cabinets, hardware, and fixtures were made to match the originals, and the counters were made of an antique English white oak. Even the stove is vintage.

ABOVE The sink in the butler's pantry was found in a restoration yard in Buffalo, New York.

LEFT In the master bedroom, an eighteenth-century English rolltop desk sits between windows hung with celadon silk curtains.

ABOVE AND BELOW The owners found the antique French fabric for the canopy at Cora Ginsburg. It was artfully hung by Gina Bianco. Paintings by Jean-François Raffaëlli frame the bed. Early nineteenth-century vases inspired by the discovery of Herculaneum and an early twentieth-century drawing adorn the mantel.

RIGHT AND BELOW For the bathrooms in the apartment, including the master bath, the owners tracked down all of the original tubs, showers, toilets, and fittings by placing an advertisement in *Old House Journal*. The double sink was original to another house from the same time period.

· 820 ·
FIFTH AVENUE

P LANS FOR 820 FIFTH AVENUE—THE THIRD LARGE APARTMENT HOUSE DEVELOPED ON the avenue—were set in motion in 1915. After 998 Fifth Avenue, completed in 1912, proved to be such a success, New York society began embracing apartment living, and speculators and investors were avidly looking for new sites. As plans and financing for a second high-class building at 907 Fifth Avenue and 72nd Street took hold, developers set their sights on the old Progress Club building on the northeast corner of 63rd Street. The Progress Club, a Jewish organization founded in 1864, had built an opulent Italian Renaissance clubhouse in 1890 that was "without doubt the most ambitious addition that has been made to the clubhouses of this city since the Union League was opened."[1] Set amid Fifth Avenue's mansions, it had lavish interiors, including a 1,000-person-capacity ballroom decorated with carved-onyx female figures adorned with electric-light tiaras. After only ten years, the club decided to relocate to the Upper West Side, and the building was sold to mining magnate James B. Haggin for $735,000. But Haggin's plans to build a new mansion never materialized. Rather, he opted to stay in his house on the corner of 64th Street and Fifth Avenue, leaving the old Progress Club vacant.

820 Fifth Avenue's investors—a group of "men of substantial financial backing" as the *New York Times* described them—were attracted by the site's choice location near 59th Street. Initially, they asked the architect Herbert Lucas to prepare designs for what was expected to be "one of the finest structures in the city," but Lucas's plans were abandoned and the commission went to Starrett & Van Vleck. Goldwin Starrett (1874–1918), an engineer and a former assistant to Daniel Burnham in Chicago, had been active in New York since 1898. He and his brothers formed the Thompson-Starrett Construction Company in 1901, and he served as the architect for the Algonquin Hotel (1902). After Ernest Van Vleck (1875–1956), a Cornell-trained architect, joined with Starrett in 1907, the firm began specializing in department stores, including Lord & Taylor on Fifth Avenue (1914) and Gimbel's in Pittsburgh (1914). 820 Fifth Avenue was its only apartment building.

Despite having little experience in high-end apartment design, Starrett & Van Vleck were successful in contributing a building with staying power. Like 998 Fifth Avenue, it was

OPPOSITE This apartment, designed by Piet Boon, includes a forty-four-foot-long gallery connecting the public rooms of the apartment. Like almost all of the rooms, its palette is stark white with black accents.

ABOVE 820 Fifth Avenue was the third high-end apartment building on the avenue. Like 998 Fifth, it was twelve stories tall and based on the Italian palazzo model.

BELOW LEFT The entrance to the lobby was understated and dignified, exuding an air of exclusivity.

BELOW RIGHT The lobby was luxuriously clad in warm, buff-colored Kasota stone and had a vaulted ceiling with Cinquecento decoration and a floor of sienna marble laid in a Cosmati design.

a great twelve-story Italian Renaissance–style limestone palazzo with symmetrical façades ornamented with restrained band courses, balconies, and window enframements and capped by a heavy overhanging cornice.[2] The reserved design was dignified and classic, lending the building a sense of solidity and permanence. Aside from two duplex maisonettes on the first and second floors, each floor housed one 6,500-square-foot apartment featuring a forty-four-foot-long stone-walled gallery lit with Italian chandeliers that connected the expansive public rooms overlooking Central Park, five bedrooms adjoined by a six-foot-wide hall, seven servants' rooms, and five fireplaces. Starrett & Van Vleck expressed the interiors as a series of formal rooms with figured American walnut floors and bold Georgian details that were reminiscent of architectural elements found in townhouses—which the new inhabitants would likely have been used to—and were equivalent in size to those of a Fifth Avenue mansion. Ceiling heights varied from floor to floor to accommodate special period decorations installed by some of the tenants and, in addition to the usual number of servants' rooms, Starrett & Van Vleck reserved a rooftop level for extra staff quarters. The lobby, too, was a luxurious selling point. Clad in warm, buff-colored Kasota stone, it featured a vaulted ceiling with Cinquecento decoration and a serpentine and sienna marble floor laid in a Cosmati design; the elevators were paneled in teak and rosewood. Originally a rental with yearly dues ranging from $18,000 to $25,000, the building changed to a cooperative in 1949.

From the beginning, 820 Fifth Avenue attracted some of the city's most prominent figures—a mix of blue-chip families, industrialists, oil barons, and the like. The building's earliest tenants included real estate scion Robert Goelet; automotive pioneer John North Willys; industrialist C. K. G. Billings; Standard Oil baron Harold I. Pratt; Mrs. Stephen V. Harkness, widow of one of Standard Oil's largest stockholders; tobacco titan George Arents; and financier and newspaper publisher Eugene Meyer. Through time, other residents have included former governor of New York Alfred E. Smith; Eberhard Faber of the Eberhard Faber Pencil Company; Alfred P. Sloane, president of General Motors; Pierre Lorillard of the well-known American tobacco family; W. Murray Crane, whose second wife, Josephine, founded the Museum of Modern Art with Abby Aldrich Rockefeller; and Mary Louise Wanamaker Munn. In the 1960s and 1970s, William Paley, head of CBS, and his trendsetting wife, Babe, resided on the ninth floor in a lavish and stylish apartment decorated by Sister Parish and Albert Hadley. Maison Jansen, fresh off of its project at the Kennedy White House, executed the architectural

details, and Billy Baldwin replicated the library he had done in the couple's former suite at the St. Regis Hotel. Oil baron Charles Wrightsman and his formidable wife, Jayne, a philanthropist and art collector, moved in in the 1950s, and Mrs. Wrightsman, now a widow, still occupies the third floor. Today, the spacious apartments remain intact and undivided, home to some of the city's most prominent businessmen and art collectors. The building continues to stand as a fortress amid the Midtown bustle, twelve mansions layered one on top of the other.

ABOVE LEFT Many of the rooms in the apartments, including this dining room, were specially designed to accommodate period decorations and architectural elements.

ABOVE RIGHT A dining room in another apartment in the building featured a tapestry on the wall and a screen.

LEFT In 1966 Cecil Beaton photographed Mrs. Charles (Jayne) Wrightsman for *Vogue*. Wearing a satin Givenchy gown, she is seated in her living room on a Louis XV cut-velvet sofa beneath Pierre-Auguste Renoir's *Girl with Cat*.

The Paley apartment was decorated by Sister Parish with architectural details by Maison Jansen. CLOCKWISE FROM TOP RIGHT The library featured fabric-covered walls and a fanciful chandelier incorporating a Moorish figure balanced atop a clock; the exuberant floral fabric on the dining room walls was echoed in the print chosen to upholster the chairs; a pedimented double door in the dining room led to the pantry; in the living room, a Pierre Bonnard still life hung above a Louis XVI chinoiserie cabinet with scarlet lacquered doors; Pablo Picasso's *Boy Leading a Horse* hung in the gallery above the eighteenth-century Italian parquet floors.

OPPOSITE Floor plan. Each floor houses one 6,500-square-foot apartment featuring a forty-four-foot-long gallery that connects the expansive public rooms overlooking Central Park, five bedrooms adjoined by a six-foot-wide hall, seven servants' rooms, and five fireplaces.

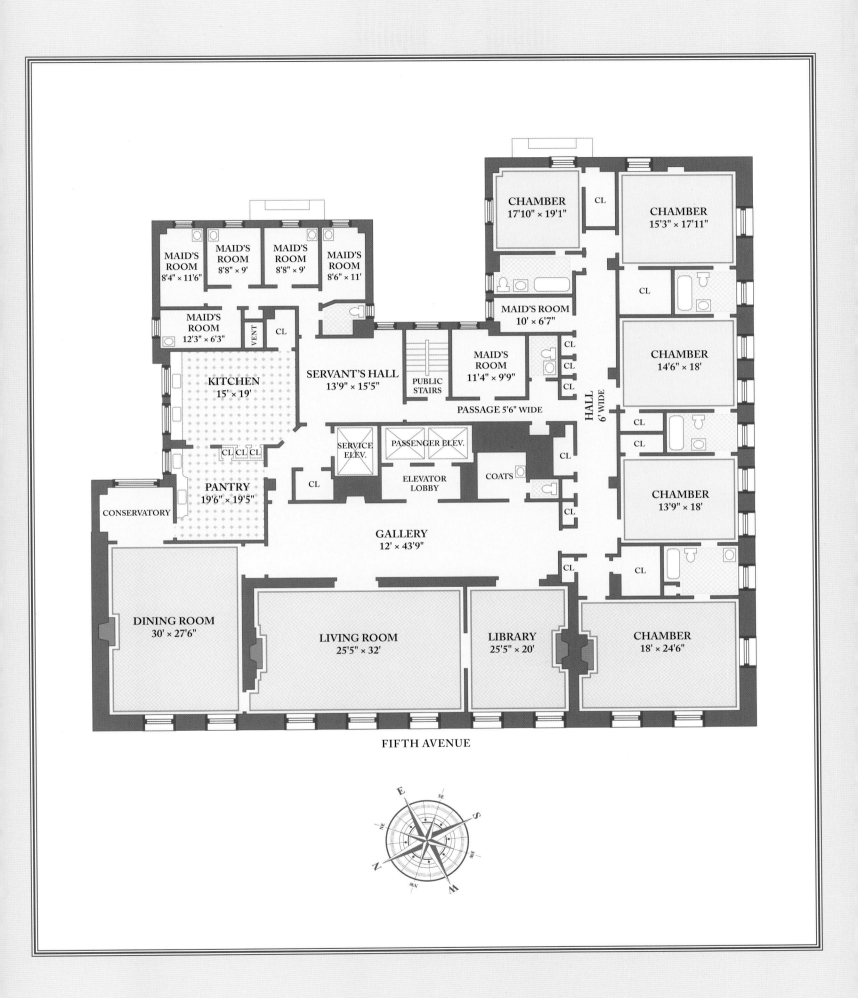

MAID'S ROOM
8'4" × 11'6"

MAID'S ROOM
8'8" × 9'

MAID'S ROOM
8'8" × 9'

MAID'S ROOM
8'6" × 11'

MAID'S ROOM
12'3" × 6'3"

VENT

CL

KITCHEN
15' × 19'

SERVANT'S HALL
13'9" × 15'5"

PUBLIC STAIRS

MAID'S ROOM
11'4" × 9'9"

PASSAGE 5'6" WIDE

CL

CL

CL

CHAMBER
17'10" × 19'1"

CL

CHAMBER
15'3" × 17'11"

CL

MAID'S ROOM
10' × 6'7"

CHAMBER
14'6" × 18'

CL

CL

HALL
6' WIDE

SERVICE ELEV.

PASSENGER ELEV.

CL CL CL

PANTRY
19'6" × 19'5"

CONSERVATORY

ELEVATOR LOBBY

COATS

CL

CHAMBER
13'9" × 18'

CL

GALLERY
12' × 43'9"

CL

CL

DINING ROOM
30' × 27'6"

LIVING ROOM
25'5" × 32'

LIBRARY
25'5" × 20'

CHAMBER
18' × 24'6"

FIFTH AVENUE

E   SE
NE   S
          SE
N   SW
   NW   W

RIGHT The living room windows overlook the park and Central Park South.

OPPOSITE Boon decorated the living room with white Flexform furniture. His minimalist aesthetic is carried through the white walls, fireplace surround, chimney breast, and flanking art.

MINIMALIST CHIC

Though some of 820's apartments retain traditional details and décor, this suite was rejuvenated in 2003 by Dutch designer Piet Boon in a fresh, contemporary style. Well-known for his minimalist aesthetic, Boon opted for a calming white palette combined with dark wood elements—ranging from furniture to doors and screens—to imbue the rooms with a meditative, almost Zen-like, tranquillity. Boon's reduced color spectrum enhances the tremendous scale of the gallery connecting the public rooms, all of which enjoy an abundance of natural light streaming in from the park. A sleek, modern kitchen incorporates Japanese-style screens and sliding doors that augment the clean, effortless chic of the design. Throughout, white-painted overscale architectural details and white upholstery punctuated with pops of blue create a sophisticated sequence of spaces that are modern and soothing.

RIGHT A suite of Christian Liaigre chairs surrounds the dining room table.

OVERLEAF LEFT The breakfast room, which originally served as the conservatory, is furnished with a Piet Boon IDS dining table and Christian Liaigre chairs.

OVERLEAF RIGHT Boon designed the kitchen with minimalist wood cabinets and natural quartz Caesarstone countertops.

PRECEDING PAGES The pristine white palette extends to the master bedroom, where a Flexform fauteuil cozies up to the fireplace.

OPPOSITE Boon embellished the ceiling of a guest room with overscale bespoke moldings. The décor includes a Piet Boon KLAAR floor lamp.

ABOVE Pops of blue bring color to a child's bedroom. Artemide Tolomeo lamps light a bed alcove.

ONE
SUTTON PLACE
SOUTH

O NE SUTTON PLACE SOUTH WAS THE FIRST LUXURY APARTMENT HOUSE TO BE built on Sutton Place—a long-neglected area of the city that was redeveloped into an exclusive colony of townhouses and upscale buildings in the 1920s. In the late 1870s, shipping merchant and entrepreneur Effingham B. Sutton (1817–1891) initially developed the riverfront stretch with brownstones, but during the intervening years the area—rife with factories, plants, and breweries—deteriorated significantly into a rundown tenement district. Real estate entrepreneur and architect Eliot Cross (1884–1949) saw the potential of the land, set high on a bluff overlooking the East River, and formed a small corporation with his brother, architect John W. Cross (1878–1951), and several other investors to buy the block between 57th and 58th Streets on what was then known as Avenue A. Successfully rebranding the area as Sutton Place, they resold the brownstones to discriminating buyers who then redeveloped them to the approval of John and Eliot's architectural firm, Cross & Cross. When Mrs. W. K. Vanderbilt decided to relocate to Sutton Place in 1921, considerable publicity and prestige descended upon the out-of-the-way corner of the city.

According to Webb & Knapp—Eliot Cross's syndicate, which grew into a sizable real estate concern later purchased by William Zeckendorf—applications for apartments from prominent New Yorkers interested in Sutton Place surged. As owner of the riverfront block between 57th and 56th Streets, the Phipps Estates—Pittsburgh steel magnate Henry Phipps's real estate arm—capitalized on the demand, commissioning Cross & Cross and the Sicilian-born Rosario Candela

OPPOSITE The fluted plaster walls in the gallery, inset with beads at the level of a traditional chair rail, create a textured backdrop for artwork and an Alberto Giacometti sculpture. The floor, inlaid with Calacatta Gold and Portoro marbles, was inspired by a traditional Roman pattern.

(1890–1953) to design a building on a par with the apartment houses that were transforming Fifth and Park Avenues. By then, Cross & Cross had distinguished themselves with designs for a series of restrained Colonial Revival clubs, houses, and apartment buildings, including the dignified and exclusive Links Club on East 64th Street and 405 Park Avenue, one of the first luxury buildings to be constructed above the tracks in the new New York Central air rights district. Candela had designed a number of solid middle-class apartment buildings on the Upper West Side since branching out on his own in

1922, but One Sutton Place South was just his second commission on the East Side. As associated architects, Candela likely designed the plans and Cross & Cross the façades; Cross & Cross were also the architects of record. By early 1925, the Burns Brothers' old frame-and-brick coal-handling plant on the site was dismantled and the Phipps Estates' new thirteen-story building was underway. As real estate broker Douglas Elliman enthusiastically remarked, "This development marks the beginning of a high-class apartment house expansion in this neighborhood."[1]

Indeed, the plans were luxurious and included such amenities as a private landscaped garden overlooking the river, an indoor tennis court beneath the garden, and a deep-water private yacht landing. The U-shaped building, comprised of two twelve- to thirteen-room simplexes and half of a twelve-room duplex per floor, allowed for views from every apartment. Conceived somewhat as a private club, some of the suites were reserved for Phipps's children, including his daughter Helen (Mrs. Bradley Martin) and his son John S. Phipps, and their friends. Phipps's other daughter, Amy, married to Frederick Guest—Winston Churchill's first cousin—took over the penthouse. Perhaps the most glamorous apartment in the city, its 6,000 square feet spread over the full footprint of the building and included two large parlors with elliptical bays, a vast wraparound terrace, and architectural fragments taken from Henry Phipps's Fifth Avenue mansion, which was torn down in 1927. Other prominent New Yorkers leased the rest of the building's thirty-five apartments, including John Sherman Hoyt, president of Columbia Presbyterian Medical Center's board of directors; publisher George P. Putnam; banker R. Thornton Wilson Jr.; industrialist H. Durant Cheever; Mrs. Paul Morton, the widow of the president of Equitable Life Assurance Society and former secretary of the Navy; and Percival Farquhar, a businessman with interests in Latin America and Russia. Vincent Astor subleased an apartment while his townhouse on East 80th Street was being built.

The building's red brick and limestone Georgian-style façades were designed in part to harmonize with the colony of Colonial Revival houses on Sutton Place. But the architects also incorporated Italian Renaissance detailing, essentially creating a great symmetrical palazzo

ABOVE A dramatically scaled porte cochere not only established a grand covered entrance to the building but also created a sense of exclusivity.

RIGHT For One Sutton Place South, Cross & Cross and Rosario Candela designed a great symmetrical palazzo with red brick and limestone Georgian-style façades and two octagonal pavilions masking water towers.

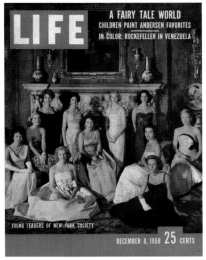

with two octagonal pavilions on the roof to mask the water towers. The dramatically scaled porte cochere established a grand entrance into the building while simultaneously maintaining a sense of exclusivity. The restrained elegance of the façades exuded refinement and dignity—an effect that Cross & Cross excelled at and were asked time and again to engineer. The lobby, featuring a wall of French doors that opened onto the private garden, was also carried out in considerable good taste.

Though One Sutton Place South spawned a series of similar buildings in the area, it has always been considered the premiere address on Sutton Place. Winston Guest, Frederick and Amy Guest's son, and his glamorous wife, C. Z., took over the penthouse. During the 1960s, socialite Marietta Tree, special ambassador to the United Nations, and her husband Ronald Tree occupied a maisonette. Betty Sherrill, the chairman of McMillen, the city's oldest and toniest interior design firm, also took up occupancy. When the East River Drive was constructed in the late 1930s, the building's garden and yacht landing were eaten up by the highway, but, happily, a deal was brokered that enabled the shareholders to lease back from the city a re-created garden on a deck that was cantilevered over the expressway. When this arrangement expired in 1990, the city and the building jockeyed over the ownership of the land, finally coming to an agreement in 2011: each entity would contribute $1 million toward the creation of a public park on a portion of the property.

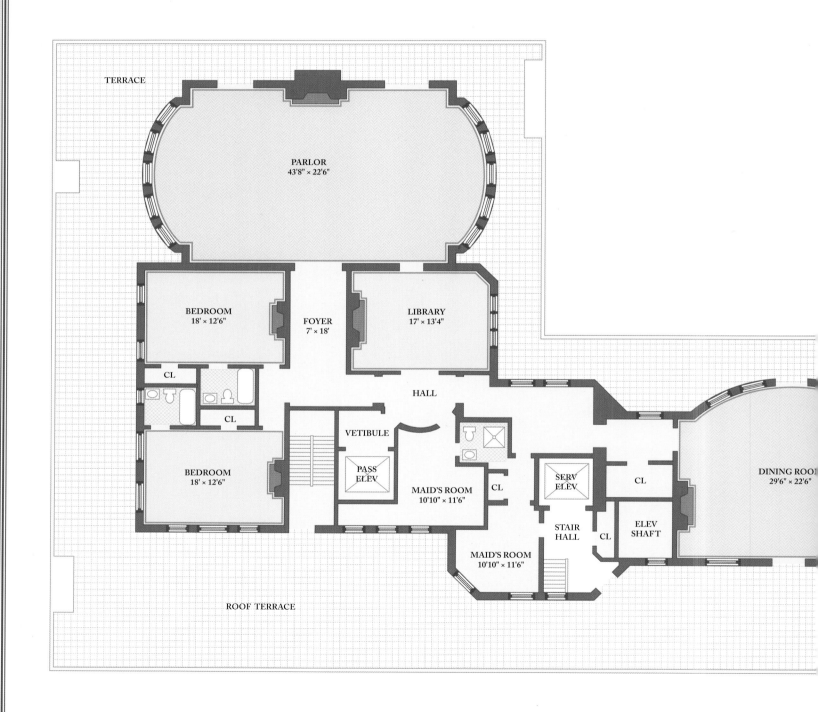

TERRACE

PARLOR
43'8" × 22'6"

BEDROOM
18' × 12'6"

FOYER
7' × 18'

LIBRARY
17' × 13'4"

CL

CL

HALL

VETIBULE

PASS
ELEV

BEDROOM
18' × 12'6"

MAID'S ROOM
10'10" × 11'6"

CL

SERV
ELEV

CL

DINING ROOM
29'6" × 22'6"

STAIR
HALL

CL

ELEV
SHAFT

MAID'S ROOM
10'10" × 11'6"

ROOF TERRACE

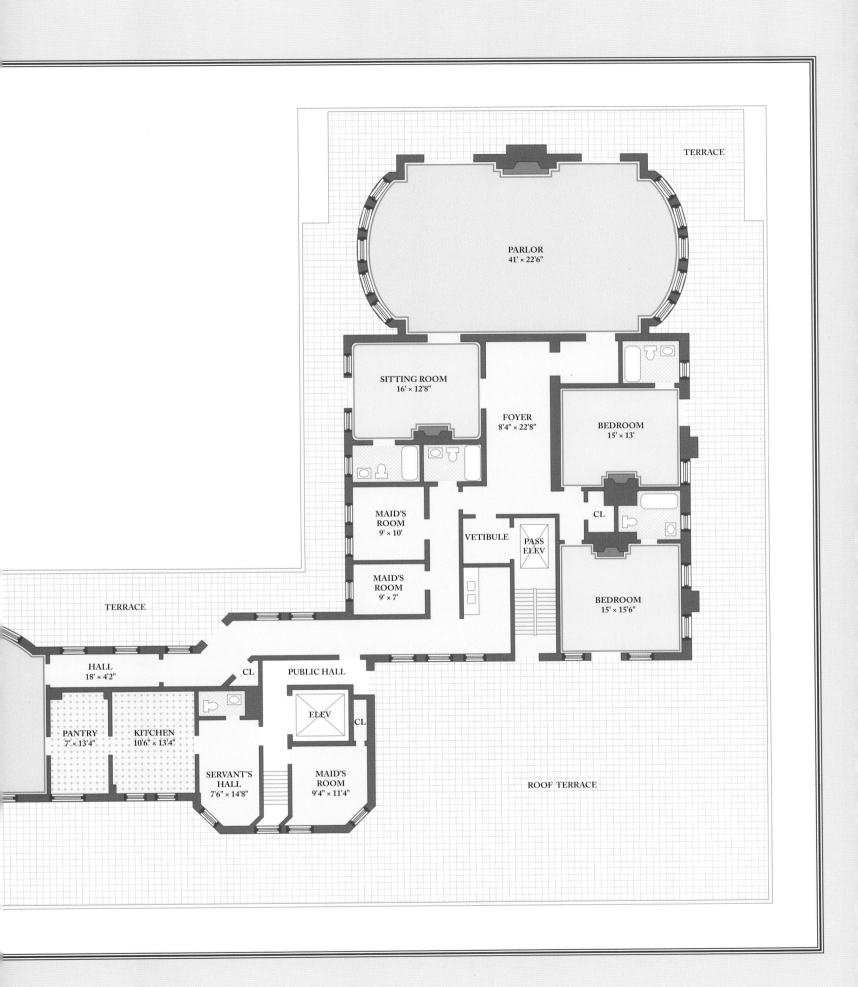

TERRACE

PARLOR
41' × 22'6"

SITTING ROOM
16' × 12'8"

FOYER
8'4" × 22'8"

BEDROOM
15' × 13'

MAID'S
ROOM
9' × 10'

VETIBULE

PASS
ELEV

CL

MAID'S
ROOM
9' × 7'

BEDROOM
15' × 15'6"

TERRACE

HALL
18' × 4'2"

CL

PUBLIC HALL

ELEV

CL

PANTRY
7' × 13'4"

KITCHEN
10'6" × 13'4"

SERVANT'S
HALL
7'6" × 14'8"

MAID'S
ROOM
9'4" × 11'4"

ROOF TERRACE

RIVERFRONT OPULENCE

In addition to exceptional views of the East River, this apartment boasts exposures to the north, south, and west—thanks to Candela's well-delineated plan—and a number of large, bright, sunlit rooms. In 2009 Peter Pennoyer Architects channeled English and Moorish influences to develop an original and stylized design aesthetic that not only showcases the owners' art collection and is glamorous enough for hosting parties but is also comfortable for daily living. A large gallery with fluted plaster walls connects the front door and foyer to the living and dining rooms, creating a sophisticated entry to the apartment's public rooms. A sumptuous palette of materials—marbles, gold and silver leaf, embossed leather, and matte gold-plated hardware—reinforces the tasteful opulence. Interior designer Michael S. Smith used luxe textiles, rich in texture and muted in color, to underscore the restrained lavishness of the design.

LEFT Brass lettering subtly announces the address of the building.

BELOW LEFT The front entrance, embellished with a broken pediment, is set within the porte cochere.

BELOW CENTER In the riverfront garden, a bench is set under a spreading cherry tree.

BELOW RIGHT Stone walls and garden urns dignify the garden.

OPPOSITE The room-like garden off of the lobby is a green oasis.

OVERLEAF The flat green lawn stretching to the East River waterfront has dramatic views of the Queensboro Bridge. Chrysanthemums and pachysandra line the lawn where it slopes down to the garden.

LEFT Paintings by Pablo Picasso decorate the living room walls. Next to the fireplace is an Empire fauteuil from Mallett.

BELOW A Matisse bronze and books sit on a coffee table by James Magni.

OPPOSITE The antique Carrara marble mantelpiece, attributed to Sir John Soane, was purchased at Chesney's.

The raised ceiling in the dining room is crowned by a gilded ellipse, from the center of which hangs an Empire chandelier from Perrin Antiquaires. Chairs from Quatrine surround a Maison Jansen table. The antique Malayer carpet complements the green silk wallcovering. Antique mirrors flanking the window reflect a collection of Impressionist paintings.

The kitchen features strapping on the ceiling and walls, a ribbed-glass and stainless-steel custom hood designed by Peter Pennoyer Architects, Calacatta Gold marble countertop and floor, a corner banquette, and a table with a tree trunk–like base by Craig Van Den Brulle.

RIGHT In the media room, a Japanese screen hangs above a Jasper sofa upholstered in a Rose Tarlow fabric.

BELOW The late nineteenth-century Chinese carpet covering the stained-oak floor in the library complements the waxed white-oak paneling and the Crillon sofa by Mattaliano.

OPPOSITE In the master bedroom, an eighteenth-century French chaise, covered in a *Lelièvre* floral-patterned fabric, occupies a sunlit corner.

RIGHT In the powder room, black-lacquered plaster stiles and rails set off Nancy Lorenz's incised, water-gilt, and burnished gold-leaf panels.

BELOW The master bedroom's walls are covered in a hand-painted paper by de Gournay and the ceiling is gold leafed. Two Swedish neoclassical mirrors from H. M. Luther flank the window on the far wall.

· 960 · FIFTH AVENUE

S LUXURIOUS BUILDINGS CONTINUED TO TRANSFORM PARK AND FIFTH AVENUES IN the 1910s and 1920s, the Italian-born Anthony Campagna (1885–1969) emerged as one of Manhattan's most prominent apartment house developers. In 1927 he organized a triad of big-name architecture firms to design 960 Fifth Avenue, perhaps the most ambitious apartment house on the thoroughfare, if not in the city, to date. He purchased the vacant mansion of the late Senator William Clark of Montana, a copper magnate, and dismantled it to make way for a "worthy successor to the townhouse." An immense and incredibly elaborate baroque confection designed by Lord, Hewlett & Hull and Henri Deglane, the 121-room Clark mansion (1907), which had cost $6 million to build, was something of a landmark—or rather a curiosity—that encapsulated the pure excess of turn-of-the-century New York. For his new speculative venture, Campagna commissioned Rosario Candela and the firm of Whitney Warren (1864–1943) and Charles Wetmore (1866–1941). Candela, the plan specialist, now riding the rise in popularity of luxury apartments, was churning out building after building, each one more spectacular than the last. Warren & Wetmore, renowned for the design of Grand Central Terminal, was an established Beaux-Arts firm responsible for creating the many offices, apartment houses, and hotels comprising Midtown's Terminal City, as well as for designing both 990 Fifth Avenue (1926) and 856 Fifth Avenue (1926) with Candela.

The design for the large and stately twelve-story limestone building was involved and spatially complex. Broken into two sections—960 Fifth Avenue and 3 East 77th Street—the building consisted of fourteen spacious cooperatives in the front and fifty-two smaller rental suites in the rear. A series of private Georgian-style dining rooms and lounges—known as the Georgian Suite—filled out the first floor. With a private entrance on 77th Street, it was serviced by a fully staffed kitchen for the building's tenants. The layouts of all but three apartments in the front portion were different; the ceiling heights and plans of simplexes and duplexes varied from floor to floor, creating an intricate web of interlocking volumes. The complex pattern of double- and single-height windows on the façade hinted at the sophistication of apartment layouts within, while Warren & Wetmore's distinctive caryatids and carved garlands adorning the cornice distinguished the roofline from afar.

OPPOSITE A Charles Le Brun *Pietà* hangs over the variegated marble mantel in the living room. Smaller works by Thomas Gainsborough and Sir David Wilkie ornament the wall to the left.

To represent the interests of the tenants, Campagna brought on Cross & Cross, architects of One Sutton Place South, as supervising architects. As the field of cooperative developments rapidly expanded, this emerging role, paid for by the builder, created a conduit—in this case, between Campagna, Candela and Warren & Wetmore, and the buyers—to produce the best possible building at the lowest possible cost. The larger and more luxurious the building, the more designers were associated with it. To further attract buyers, society decorator Dorothy Draper was called upon to collaborate on all of the public halls and lounges, including the restaurant and large dining suite. "While a great deal of sentiment is attached to the old historic mansions along Fifth Avenue," remarked real estate specialist Roland F. Elliman in 1929, "there should be a feeling of exultation when a beautiful structure such as 960 Fifth Avenue exemplifying the last word in modern architectural design and sumptuous interior appointments replaces a private residential dwelling."[1]

Clearly, Campagna's no-holds-barred approach toward speculative building worked—all fourteen suites sold as the building neared completion, garnering some of the highest prices ever paid at that time. Seventy-five percent of the building was sold even before the frame was enclosed. In June 1927 Dr. Preston Pope Satterwhite purchased an eighteen-room duplex apartment, including the celebrated double-height salon that occupied the center bay on the tenth floor of the building, for a record price of $450,000. Financier and famous horseman James Cox Brady's duplex penthouse suite contained twenty-four rooms. In February 1929 lawyer Augustine L. Humes bought the last apartment available, a thirteen-room duplex. As the building neared completion, a critic from the *New Yorker* toured the building and marveled at its magnificence, writing: "The floors were deep in plaster and lath the day we were there, whistling workmen shuffled about, and a plinth for an agate lamp or a marble figure supported only an empty milk bottle. But the grandeur of the place could be foreseen. The ceiling of the living room [of the Satterwhite apartment] is twenty-two feet high and tall windows reach to within two feet of it. Nothing was lacking to make it seem like a hall at Versailles except the playing of silver fountains in the panorama below. The crowning glory of this same building is a penthouse [Brady apartment] with eighteen rooms [*sic*]. We were duly awed, even though we rode up to it in a work elevator with two wheelbarrows filled with sand. It flaunts defiance to the proud adjacent skyline, which meets the challenge, so far as our eye could see, with nothing nearly so immense."[2]

LEFT The complex pattern of single- and double-height windows on the façade hint at the sophisticated apartment layouts within, while a row of distinctive caryatids and a string of carved garlands distinguish the roofline of the building.

RIGHT 960 Fifth replaced the mansion of the late Senator William Clark of Montana, a copper magnate who built an extravagant 121-room baroque confection on the site in 1907.

In contrast to the tastes of the prior generation, as exemplified by the Clark mansion, the inhabitants of 960 Fifth desired a more refined, less ostentatious expression of their wealth. The Georgian-style interiors—in the Georgian Suite, the lobby, and the apartments—exuded the quintessence of subdued dignity. Over time, other residents, including Mrs. Henry "Sister" Parish, Claus and Sunny von Bülow, John Drexel, Ailsa Mellon Bruce, and Edgar Bronfman Sr., have enjoyed 960's refined and gracious apartments. Even John Cross, of the architectural duo Cross & Cross, who worked on the building, had faith in its design, landing there as a resident himself in the 1940s. Today, most of the expansive original layouts remain, but some apartments, such as the Satterwhites' and a four-story maisonette with its own entrance on Fifth Avenue, have been divided. The building continues to offer the best of the best in amenities. In addition to dining in the in-house restaurant, residents can take meals in their apartments prepared by the building's French chef—one of only three private building chefs on Fifth Avenue. An elaborate rooftop gym commands views of Central Park. The apartments at 3 East 77th Street, built originally as the rental portion, continue as the ultimate New York cooperative pied-à-terre, benefiting from the same perks and creature comforts as the front apartments. The building's superintendent—dapperly clad in a coat and tie—operates much in the capacity of a club manager, presiding over the rarified world of 960 Fifth.

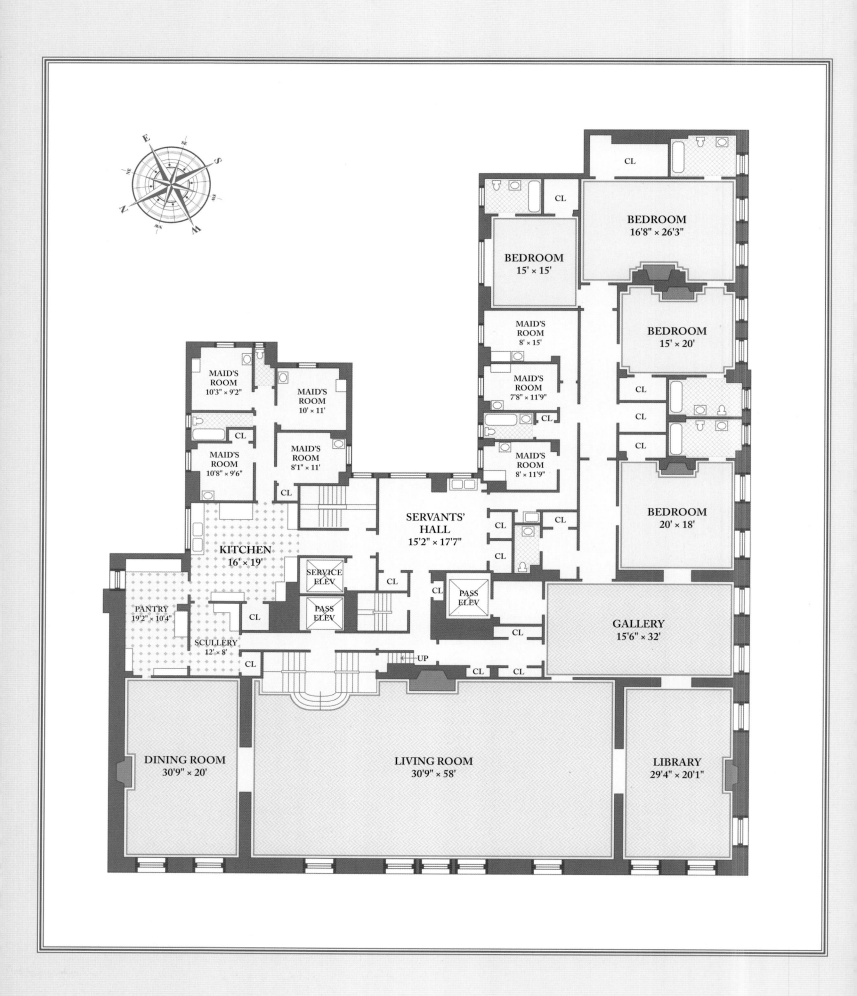

MAID'S ROOM
10'3" × 9'2"

MAID'S ROOM
10' × 11'

MAID'S ROOM
10'8" × 9'6"

MAID'S ROOM
8'1" × 11'

CL

CL

CL

KITCHEN
16' × 19'

PANTRY
19'2" × 10'4"

SCULLERY
12' × 8'

SERVICE ELEV

PASS ELEV

CL

CL

CL

CL

SERVANTS'
HALL
15'2" × 17'7"

MAID'S ROOM
8' × 15'

MAID'S ROOM
7'8" × 11'9"

CL

MAID'S ROOM
8' × 11'9"

CL

CL

CL

CL

CL

PASS ELEV

CL

UP

CL

CL

BEDROOM
15' × 15'

CL

CL

BEDROOM
16'8" × 26'3"

BEDROOM
15' × 20'

CL

CL

CL

CL

BEDROOM
20' × 18'

GALLERY
15'6" × 32'

DINING ROOM
30'9" × 20'

LIVING ROOM
30'9" × 58'

LIBRARY
29'4" × 20'1"

MUSEUM MILE MASTERPIECE

The spacious proportions of the public rooms and the stair hall in this duplex are indicative of the scale of all of the apartments in the building: they are rooms designed for entertaining and to display art. From the stair railings and moldings to the marble mantelpieces and arched doorways, the architectural details and quiet elegance of the spaces evoke the glory of the 1920s apartment era. Now the rooms are filled with a highly varied collection of art, ranging from the Italian Renaissance to today. The generous foyer and stair hall double as a gallery, and the wood-paneled dining room is designed to showcase a collection of Italian Renaissance paintings and religious art. Upstairs, the deep pink silk-covered walls of the living room display a number of smaller landscapes by various English and Welsh artists, among others. In contrast, the more contemporary media room, its walls covered in leather studded with a grid of nailheads, aptly features much more recent art.

OPPOSITE Floor plan. The Satterwhite apartment occupied the entire tenth floor of the building and included a large entrance gallery, a dining room, living room, and library arranged in an enfilade, extensive staff quarters, and four large bedrooms. From the living room, stairs led up to the master suite on the eleventh floor.

ABOVE On the upper level of the duplex, the stair landing features paintings by Max Beckmann.

OVERLEAF The expansive foyer doubles as a gallery space, showcasing the work of Carracci, Joseph Michael Gandy, Anne-Louis Girodet de Roussy-Trioson, James Ward, and Richard Wilson.

PRECEDING PAGES The deep pink silk of the living room's walls
sets off a series of paintings by Richard Parkes Bonington.

ABOVE The living room also features Guercino's *St. John the Baptist in the Wilderness*, ca. 1652–55, above the sideboard. Beautifully framed paintings by Richard Wilson, Moses van Uyttenbroeck, Giovanni Lanfranco, Gerard Seghers, Goffredo Wals, Samuel Palmer, and Bonington line the walls.

ABOVE LEFT AND LEFT In the dining room, a collection of gold-ground paintings of religious subjects is artfully arranged within cabinets to striking effect. Scenes of the Virgin, the Nativity, various saints, the Crucifixion, and the Resurrection by a range of fourteenth- and fifteenth-century artists are well preserved in this temperature- and humidity-controlled space.

The dining room is a shrine to the Italian Renaissance. In addition to the gold-ground paintings, the well-lit, paneled cabinets display artifacts and vessels. Annibale Carraci's *Virgin and Child with Saint Lucy and the Young Saint John the Baptist*, ca. 1587–88, has pride of place over the mantel.

ABOVE The kitchen's sleek stainless-steel cabinets are in striking contrast to the traditional wood floor.

OPPOSITE TOP The family room features a suede sofa, animal-print carpet, leather walls studded with a grid of nailheads, and Peter Saul's *Name That Tune*, 2007.

OPPOSITE BOTTOM A Ray Johnson collage hangs above an upright piano.

·720·
PARK AVENUE

IN 1928, PLANS FOR A NEW $6 MILLION COOPERATIVE APARTMENT BUILDING ON THE CREST of Lenox Hill were announced. When the Presbyterian Hospital—once located on the block bound by 70th and 71st Streets and Park and Madison Avenues—decided to relocate to a new campus in Washington Heights in the mid-1920s, its site was freed up for prime residential development. With real estate prices increasing, investors Robert E. Dowling and James T. Lee—the man behind 998 Fifth Avenue—along with architects Eliot Cross and J. E. R. Carpenter, purchased the site in 1925 and resold it soon thereafter to Harby, Abrons & Melius for a tidy profit of $2 million. In 1928 it switched hands again and was broken into four sections: the Madison Avenue frontage, which sold to the Tishman family; two large lots facing Park Avenue; and seven mid-block sites on 70th and 71st Streets for private houses backing onto a private garden.

Jesse Isidor Straus (1872–1936), a prominent Jew and Harvard-educated president of R. H. Macy & Co., purchased the northwest corner of 70th Street and Park Avenue and developed the luxurious 720 Park Avenue; he was also responsible for 730 Park Avenue next door.[1] Straus's grandparents had emigrated from Otterberg, Germany, in the 1850s, first settling in Georgia, where they opened a dry goods store. When the Strauses relocated to New York in 1865, they opened L. Straus & Sons, importers of glass and china, with a branch in the basement of Macy's on 14th Street. By 1884, the Strauses owned part of the company and by 1896, they had become sole owners of R. H. Macy & Co. A prominent figure in the civic and philanthropic life of the city, Straus's father, Isidor—who died aboard the ill-fated *Titanic*—founded the Educational Alliance for immigrants and represented New York's 15th District in Congress.

Jesse Straus's syndicate, the Montelenox Corporation, headed by Alfred Selisberg, commissioned Eliot Cross and his brother John of Cross & Cross and Rosario Candela—the architectural team that had recently worked on One Sutton Place South and 960 Fifth Avenue—to design the building. Earmarking some of the suites for himself and his family, Straus sought to create lavish quarters where his friends and colleagues would be welcome. Straus believed in having his family around him; all three of his children had apartments in the building. As his grandson Ken Straus recalled, the building "might well have been called the Straus Family Apartment Building."[2] The apartments were

OPPOSITE A custom Wilton carpet by Colefax and Fowler lines the elegantly curved stair. The stairwell wall is hung with dozens of small drawings and paintings, installed by Frank Keller.

planned expansively. As the *New York Times* reported, "Preliminary plans indicate that the projected apartments will in many ways reach a new level in size and beauty."[3]

As in many of their shared commissions, Cross & Cross designed the façades and Candela the floor plans. Cross & Cross enhanced the Renaissance-inspired brick façades with limestone quoins, balustrades, and a base embellished with delicately carved festoons of flowers and fruit. The building's first twelve stories ascended squarely in accordance with the Park Avenue street wall, but the top six floors' cascading setbacks, terraces, and Tudor-style bays drew the ire of *The New Yorker*'s architectural critic T-Square, prompting him to write that the building was "quite a disturbing pile of architectural motives." Although "it begins its upward career in an orderly fashion," he found that above the "main cornice, the building breaks out in a jumble of setbacks, stick-outs, bays, battlements and buttresses. Doubtless these create numerous amusing little roof spaces but as a design they are rather incoherent."[4] Despite

ABOVE The Renaissance-inspired building rises conventionally to the twelfth floor, after which it ascends asymmetrically in a series of setbacks, terraces, and bays.

RIGHT George McNeir's apartment featured an array of Spanish and Italian details.

BELOW LEFT Frederic H. Frazier, chairman of the General Baking Company, opted for formal Georgian-style interiors in his sixteenth-floor apartment.

BELOW RIGHT Banker Francis M. Weld's apartment included a conservatory off of the dining room.

the criticism of the building's design, the dramatic upper floors were to become a hallmark of Candela's work—celebrated artistic gestures all along Fifth and Park Avenues.

Straus's venture was successful; with four months to completion, 83 percent of the suites had been sold. Starrett Brothers, who went on to build the Empire State Building, officially completed 720 Park Avenue the day before the stock market crashed in October 1929. Each of the lower stories featured one vast apartment with a forty-foot-long gallery and half of a duplex level to the west. On the upper floors, the cascading setbacks contained several sprawling duplexes, some of which had eighteen rooms, terraces, three exposures, and

conservatories. The lobby consisted of a series of gracious Georgian-style rooms with a comfortable club-like ambience, an atmosphere further enhanced by the private squash court, which Straus specified for the basement and which still exists. In addition to the Strauses, early occupants were a mix of business executives and bankers. Straus, who would go on to serve as the U.S. ambassador to France from 1933 to 1936, moved into a seven-bedroom duplex on the twelfth and thirteenth floors that included a mezzanine level for servants' quarters. The interiors reflected the Strauses' varied tastes: the living room and stone-trimmed gallery, decorated with fine religious paintings, were Italian in style, the dining room and library were English in spirit, and Irma Straus's bedroom and boudoir were French. The Strauses' son Jack and his family occupied a duplex on the eighth and ninth floors; their son Robert Kenneth had an Art Deco–themed bachelor pad on the twelfth floor; and their daughter, Beatrice, and her family lived in an eighth-floor apartment in the front of the building. George McNeir, chairman of Mohawk Carpet Mills, asked the decorator Herbert Abbott to embellish his apartment with an array of Spanish and Italian details such as hand-painted ceilings and a wrought-iron Florentine gate to separate the gallery from the bedroom hall. Frederic H. Frazier, chairman of the General Baking Company, opted for more formal Georgian décor in his sixteenth-floor apartment. Thomas Ewing Jr., president of Alexander Smith and Sons Carpet Company in Yonkers, took a duplex on the thirteenth and fourteenth floors. Other residents included bankers Francis M. Weld and Harold Russell Ryder, manufacturer Jonathan Godfrey, capitalist William E. Iselin, automobile manufacturer Walter P. Chrysler, and Mary dePeyster Cary. Today, 720 Park Avenue continues to boast some of Manhattan's most impressive apartments and is largely occupied by business executives and New Yorkers prominent in city life.

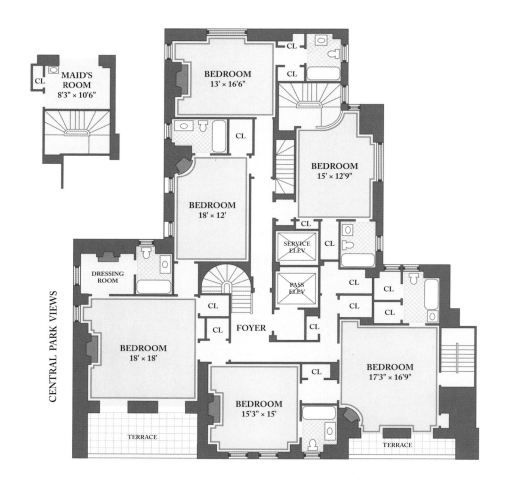

CENTRAL PARK VIEWS

MAID'S ROOM
8'3" × 10'6"

BEDROOM
13' × 16'6"

BEDROOM
18' × 12'

BEDROOM
15' × 12'9"

CL

SERVICE ELEV

PASS ELEV

DRESSING ROOM

BEDROOM
18' × 18'

FOYER

BEDROOM
17'3" × 16'9"

BEDROOM
15'3" × 15'

TERRACE

TERRACE

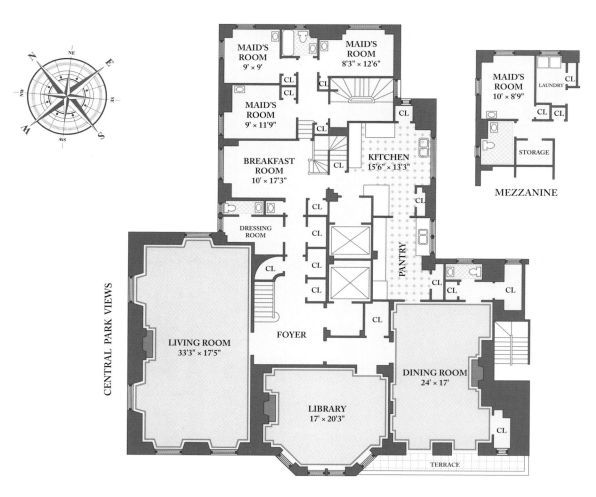

CENTRAL PARK VIEWS

MAID'S ROOM
9' × 9'

MAID'S ROOM
8'3" × 12'6"

MAID'S ROOM
9' × 11'9"

BREAKFAST ROOM
10' × 17'3"

KITCHEN
15'6" × 13'3"

MAID'S ROOM
10' × 8'9"

LAUNDRY

STORAGE

MEZZANINE

DRESSING ROOM

PANTRY

LIVING ROOM
33'3" × 17'5"

FOYER

DINING ROOM
24' × 17'

LIBRARY
17' × 20'3"

TERRACE

OPPOSITE Floor plan. A duplex on the fifteenth and sixteenth floors in the western wing of the building features terraces and bays built into the setbacks and mezzanine levels. The living room and master bedroom overlook Central Park.

ABOVE The architectural treatment of the upper floors of the building is a hallmark of architect Rosario Candela's work.

CANDELA DUPLEX

Over the past thirty years, the owners of this charming duplex have continued to refresh and refine their family home. When they purchased the apartment in the 1980s, they upgraded the mechanical systems, kitchen, and bathrooms, untouched since 1929, and combined several servants' rooms—complete with a dumbwaiter to the kitchen below—into larger secondary bedrooms and baths. By cleaning, refinishing, and painting the apartment's original boiserie and paneling, they were able to highlight the distinctive architectural character of the public rooms. Vivien Greenock, formerly of Colefax and Fowler, carried out the interiors over a period of ten years in the 1980s and 1990s, and aspects of her hand are still visible, particularly in the library and master bedroom. Katie Ridder, well known for her exuberant and colorful décor, refreshed the dining and living rooms and upstairs study. The owners—inspired by a visit to the Duke of Windsor's house in the Bois de Boulogne—accentuated the living room's delicate French boiserie with blue and silver gilding. Subsequently, Tom Scheerer, renowned for his fresh, well-edited designs, redecorated many of the rooms upstairs. In addition to the ornate paneling, the spacious 7,000-square-foot apartment abounds in original detail, including four marble mantelpieces and wide-plank oak floors. But the owners have added new elements—such as the bookshelves lining the second-floor gallery—that blend seamlessly with the old. With an eclectic mix of antiques and contemporary furnishings, the rooms are colorful, stylish, and homey. The curved stair ascending from the foyer to the upstairs gallery is the centerpiece of the apartment. The stairwell is hung with dozens of small drawings and paintings—anniversary and birthday gifts accumulated over time—expertly installed by Frank Keller.

TOP Cross & Cross's elaborate stone moldings define the base of the building.

ABOVE The doors and fanlight of the arched entrance feature organic wrought-iron details.

OVERLEAF Hand-blocked Colefax and Fowler wallpaper lining the walls of the front hall is the backdrop for a George II marble-topped parcel-gilt console and a pair of Moroccan baluster jar lamps.

PAGES 124–25 In the living room, interior designer Katie Ridder added upholstered sofas, a bridgewater chair covered in a Larsen fabric, side tables custom made by David Melchior, and an Edelman shagreen coffee table custom made by Urban, all of which blend harmoniously with a late nineteenth-century Axminster carpet and Kangxi-era Coromandel screen.

OPPOSITE TOP LEFT
A Georgian walnut card table
is decorated with trompe
l'oeil needlepoint.

OPPOSITE TOP RIGHT
The blue and silver gilding of
the living room's distinctive
French boiserie was inspired
by the Duke of Windsor's
salon in the Bois de Boulogne.
A Walter Gay interior hangs
over a Régence walnut console,
on which rests a Jules Dalou
bronze portrait bust.

OPPOSITE BOTTOM A sofa at one
end of the room is upholstered in
orange Henry Calvin linen.

RIGHT In the music room,
which connects to the living
room, a Louis XVI black-and-
gilt *bureau plat* has pride of place.

BELOW Ridder refreshed the
music room with a custom
sofa and a pair of club chairs,
all upholstered in fabric from
Holland & Sherry, and curtains
in rose pink silk velvet from
Bergamo Fabrics.

LEFT AND ABOVE The Colefax and Fowler rug in the dining room is complemented by curtains in a Bruschwig & Fils taffeta embroidered by Penn & Fletcher in a design by Ridder. Chairs from Carlton House Restoration with burnt orange Edelman leather seats and arms bring out the same color in the rug. A Rajasthani portrait hangs above a black-and-gilt side table.

LEFT Vivien Greenock decorated the intimate library in soft shades of yellow with red accents.

BELOW In a corner of the library, a group of Delft vases is combined with a still life by Harry Bloomfield.

OPPOSITE An arch on the top of the landing, designed by Nancy and John Beringer to echo the one on the floor below, lends definition to the space. They also designed the gallery bookcase.

Ridder covered the walls
of the upstairs TV room in
Brunschwig & Fils's Kitchen
Garden linen and added a
bridgewater sofa upholstered
in a Castel fabric.

A brass-and-steel four-poster,
designed by Tom Scheerer,
is the centerpiece of one of
the upstairs bedrooms, which
Scheerer decorated.

LEFT A collection of decoupage vases decorates a painted Provençal table in the master bedroom.

BELOW The master bedroom furniture is upholstered in Pompadour linen from Christopher Moore.

The richly ornamented boiserie of the overdoors and the canopy-like extension over the bed create an elegant setting for an array of French botanical lithographs.

NEW WINE IN OLD BOTTLES

BELOW A Jean Prouvé table decorated with African wedding headdresses collected by the owner stands in the center of the front hall. The walls, plastered in bands of textured and smooth finish, are hung with works by Ed Ruscha and Robert Mapplethorpe.

OPPOSITE A highly polished steel chair by Joel Morrison from the Gagosian Gallery sits next to the entrance to the dining room.

This bright and airy simplex, decorated by Jamie Tisch, revolves around an expansive gallery that packs a powerful punch. Though it retains its original black-and-white marble floor, its walls are plastered in bands of textured and smooth finish and lined with bold contemporary art and photography by modern-day heavyweights Robert Mapplethorpe, Ed Ruscha, Vera Lutter, David Benjamin Sherry, and Joel Morrison. The entertaining rooms unfold in an enfilade and are divided by vibrant red pocket doors. The cozy wood-paneled library, bright white living room, and dining room with burlap-covered walls feature a well-edited mix of comfortable and chic furnishings by such mid-century designers as Jean Prouvé, Josef Hoffmann, and Jacques Adnet. And whereas many of the original architectural details of the apartment have been updated—apart from the library's distinctive wood paneling—the new moldings and mantelpieces honor the scale and traditional quality of Candela's interiors. Throughout, lively art and photography by the likes of Marilyn Minter, Alex Katz, and Enoc Perez comingle with vintage furniture and contemporary pieces in a vivacious and colorful mix of old and new. A number of bedrooms, a large kitchen, and service spaces round out the floor plan, which also includes a mezzanine level secreted away by the kitchen. A stylish family apartment, its rooms not only abound in visual interest but are also comfortable and inviting.

PRECEDING PAGES The burlap covering the dining room walls sets off a painting by Enoc Perez. Blue-and-white vintage vases decorate the mantel and echo the Prussian blue velvet of the chairs, once owned by the Thurn und Taxis family and acquired from Mallett Antiques. The tablecloth is a Raoul fabric.

ABOVE An antique carpet anchors the décor of the living room. A painting by Marilyn Minter hangs over the mantel. Irish crystal-framed mirrors from O'Sullivan Antiques and a pair of Samuel Marx parchment-clad chests flank the red-lacquered doors into the library. Custom-made curtains by Colombian artist Jorge Elizondo for Hechizoo hang at the windows, and a Paula Hayes terrarium decorates the coffee table.

ABOVE right An ebony chair with ivory inlay from Keil's Antiques in New Orleans is paired with a vintage Murano-glass sconce from Lucca Antiques.

RIGHT Italian silver objects and a bouquet of flowers decorate a tortoiseshell table from Gracie.

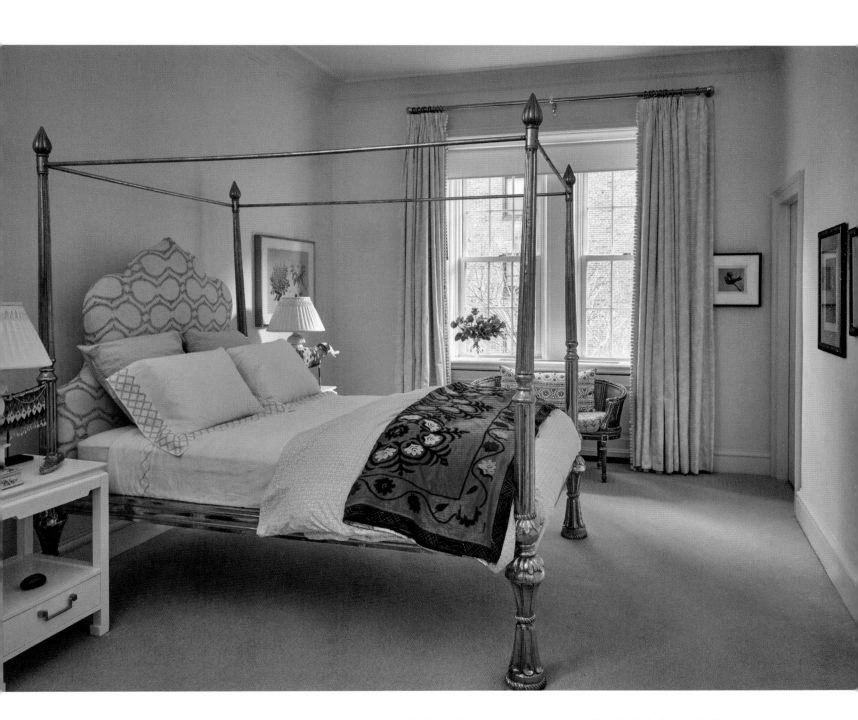

OPPOSITE top In the library, an Alex Katz painting hangs above a pair of leather chairs by Josef Hoffmann. A vintage French side table and a Jean Royère floor lamp sit to the left of the sofa, which is upholstered in a Cowtan & Tout corduroy.

OPPOSITE BOTTOM In the kitchen, marble walls, tabletops, and countertops set off the gray cabinets from SieMatic. Soane light fixtures hang above the island.

ABOVE In a child's bedroom, the four-poster's headboard and linens are by John Robshaw. The coverlet is a vintage Suzani. The curtain fabric is by Ralph Lauren and the carpet is from Patterson Flynn Martin. Works by Andy Warhol and William Wegman decorate the walls.

ABOVE In the master bedroom, the Bennison fabric Songbird is used for the walls and the canopy of the bed. A Schumacher taffeta lines the canopy. Vintage Murano-glass lamps from Downtown in Los Angeles flank the bed.

LEFT A vintage mirror from O'Sullivan Antiques reflects an Albert Bierstadt painting and Jacques Adnet lamp.

OPPOSITE A painting by Rufino Tamayo hangs on the far wall. The curtains are a Manuel Canovas fabric and the sheets are by Porthault.

THE BERESFORD

I N 1928—ON THE EVE OF THE DEPRESSION—ARCHITECT EMERY ROTH (1871–1948) WAS awarded one of the most important commissions of his career, the Beresford on Central Park West. He had come a long way from his impoverished beginnings as a thirteen-year-old Austro-Hungarian emigrant, and the building stands as one of his crowning achievements.

As a young and talented designer, Roth first found employment in Chicago at Burnham & Root working on the 1893 Columbian Exposition. After relocating to New York, he successively joined the offices of Richard Morris Hunt and Ogden Codman. In the 1910s and 1920s, Roth forged a name for himself with a series of well-planned, luxurious apartment buildings on the Upper East and Upper West Sides, most with Italian Renaissance–style detailing. His Ritz Tower (1925–27) at 465 Park Avenue, designed with Carrère & Hastings, won acclaim as the first residential skyscraper with terraces incorporated into the setbacks. With the Oliver Cromwell (1927) at 18 West 72nd Street and, after the Beresford, the San Remo (1930) at 145–46 Central Park West and the Eldorado (1931) at 300 Central Park West, Roth cemented his mastery of the luxury apartment tower—distinctively detailed, iconic silhouettes against the New York sky.

As the *New York Times* noted in 1928, "A new residential thoroughfare is being developed [that] will equal Park and Fifth Avenues on the East Side. It is Central Park West which is beginning to show very marked evidences of a great building revival and which will provide some of the finest and best equipped apartment houses for well-to-do and discerning tenants."[1] The fact that Central Park West did not have the same cachet as its East Side counterparts did not hold real estate developers and speculators back from transforming the avenue into an impressive line of architecturally distinct buildings, all fifteen stories in height. In 1928 the newly widened and paved avenue was emerging from years of disruptive subway construction, and its potential as a park-front stretch was starting to be re-realized some forty years after the construction of the Dakota. Between 82nd and 92nd Streets, six new buildings had recently been completed and six more were in the pipeline. As one real estate expert commented, "In its early development twenty to twenty-five years ago, Central Park West established new standards of apartments for that time" with the Dakota and other buildings of its type. "Now," he continued, "this west side boulevard is coming back to claim its former preeminence."[2]

OPPOSITE Octagonal, copper-roofed towers anchor three corners of the building and create the Beresford's iconic presence in the skyline.

The Beresford Hotel, a two-part building consisting of a six-story and a ten-story section, had occupied the site of the present-day Beresford since about 1889 and had been part of Central Park West's first building boom. The low-rise structures, along with several brownstones on West 81st Street, presented an opportunity: a large, improvable lot unhemmed in by tall buildings. In 1927 Max Verschleiser purchased the hotel for $2 million and commissioned Roth to modernize the building for $300,000. However, it appears that by 1928, the property had been taken over by Manhattan Square Beresford, Inc., headed by Hyman Lipschultz, and Roth's plan had become more ambitious. Commanding frontage on two major Upper West Side arteries, the site overlooked both Central Park and Manhattan Square, occupied by the low-lying American Museum of Natural History. In August 1928 Roth filed plans for yet another fifteen-story building on the almost square footprint (204 by 185 feet), estimated to cost $3,650,000.

Spanning the entire block front between 81st and 82nd Streets, the Beresford was the largest apartment house in the city at the time of its completion in 1930. When finished, the limestone and buff-colored-brick building rose to twenty-two stories, instead of fifteen. And though the U-shaped structure was expansive, the openness of the site absorbed its immense bulk. Roth created the impression of a great fortress with three octagonal, copper-roofed towers anchoring the three corners of the building visible from the major streets. To counterbalance the building's monumentality, Roth gave it an air of luxury and intimate exclusivity at street level. Instead of one large lobby, he designed three separate marble-clad lobbies and entrances—one on Central Park West and two on West 81st Street—which fed into five elevator banks. In effect, the building was three buildings in one, and tenants shared semiprivate elevator landings with, at most, one other apartment per floor. The lower levels contained ten apartments, but on the upper floors, where setbacks formed an array of terraces and outdoor aeries, there were fewer apartments and more luxurious duplexes were introduced. All of the apartments had at least one wood-burning fireplace, and though Roth held back on interior architectural embellishment, the spacious, light-filled rooms had lofty ceilings and extraordinary views.

ABOVE LEFT Most of the Beresford's apartments were leased from plans and drawings, including this 1928 rendering of the building.

ABOVE RIGHT The old Beresford Hotel, built ca. 1889, consisted of a six-story and a ten-story section. It occupied the site of the present-day Beresford and was part of the first wave of building on Central Park West.

BELOW The living room of banker Maurice S. Benjamin's apartment featured distinctive wood paneling, including a carved panel over the fireplace, November 1, 1930.

Roth did not restrain himself on the façades, however, creating a giant palazzo with judiciously applied ornament and architectural embellishment. As noted by the *New York Times*, "The Beresford has set a new standard on the west side in apartment-house rentals and this high standard also applies to the entire equipment and structural finish of the building."[3] Architectural flourishes, including string courses, rustification, balustrades, and carved details at key moments, enhanced the grandeur of the exterior, and the cascading terraces and embellished towers added to its impact on the skyline. Though all the apartments were well appointed and generously sized, the three tower apartments represented the building's prime real estate. Multilevel townhouses in the sky, each boasted a series of terraces with panoramic views and a large octagonal room with seventeen-foot ceilings and huge arched windows.

Before its completion, the building began to fill rapidly, most of the apartments having been leased from architect's plans. In September 1929, the *New York Times* reported that "of the 178 suites in the building there are now but eleven vacancies and more than half, if not all, of these are likely to be rented before Oct. 1."[4] Twenty percent of the tenants relocated from the East Side. Real estate developer Irving S. Chanin leased a terrace apartment while working on his new building, the Majestic, six blocks south, and cosmetics entrepreneur Helena Rubinstein rented a duplex on the 21st and 22nd floors. Other notable early residents included Nathan Straus Jr., a former state senator; Leo Fischer, president of the Thompson-Starrett Company; Julian Henry Cohen, counsel of the Port Authority; and William C. Beschorman, vice president of the National Lead Company. At first, the building attracted upper-class Jews, some of whom would not have been admitted to the high-end buildings across the park. Over time, a variety of actors, performers, and other creative types, including the opera singer Beverly Sills, actors Rock Hudson and Tony Randall, editor Helen Gurley Brown, singer Diana Ross, and comedian Jerry Seinfeld, have called the Beresford home. Only at the Beresford would you find the violinist Isaac Stern and lyricist and playwright Adolph Green sharing an elevator landing— in the 1990s, they lived in side-by-side duplexes on upper floors overlooking the park.

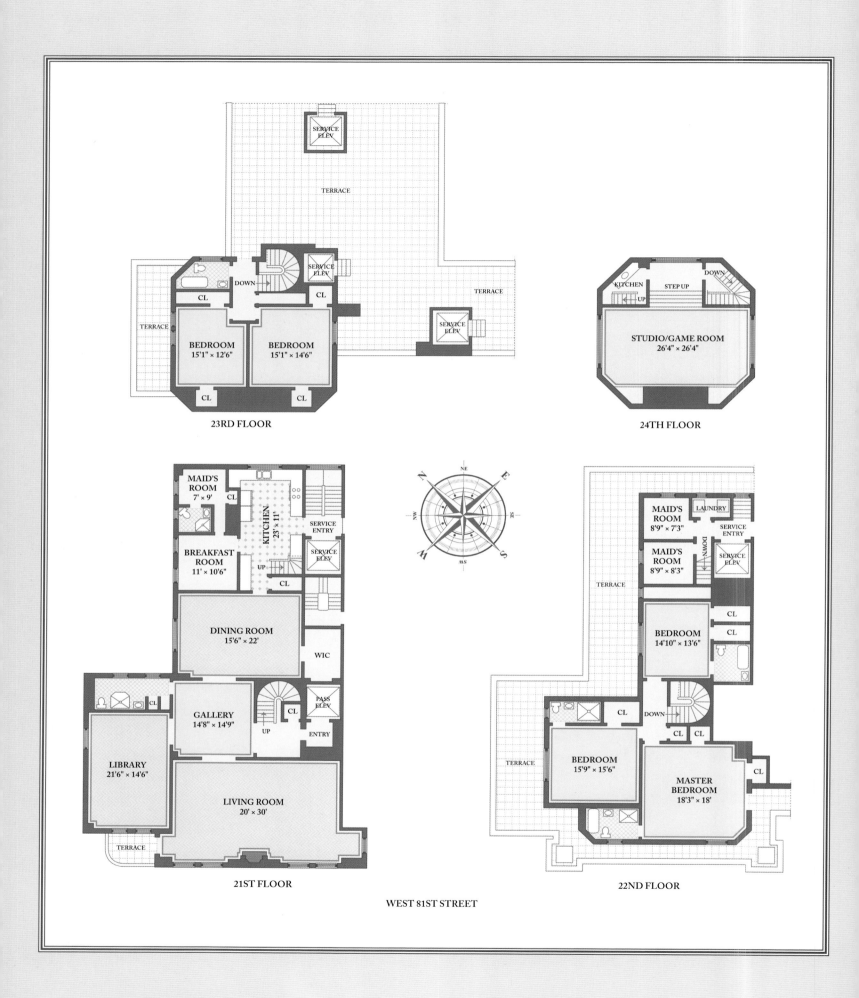

23RD FLOOR

SERVICE ELEV

TERRACE

TERRACE

DOWN

CL

CL

TERRACE

BEDROOM
15'1" × 12'6"

BEDROOM
15'1" × 14'6"

SERVICE ELEV

CL

CL

24TH FLOOR

KITCHEN

STEP UP

DOWN

UP

STUDIO/GAME ROOM
26'4" × 26'4"

21ST FLOOR

MAID'S ROOM
7' × 9'

CL

KITCHEN
23' × 11'

SERVICE ENTRY

SERVICE ELEV

BREAKFAST ROOM
11' × 10'6"

CL

UP

DINING ROOM
15'6" × 22'

WIC

LIBRARY
21'6" × 14'6"

CL

GALLERY
14'8" × 14'9"

CL

PASS ELEV

UP

ENTRY

LIVING ROOM
20' × 30'

TERRACE

22ND FLOOR

MAID'S ROOM
8'9" × 7'3"

LAUNDRY

SERVICE ENTRY

MAID'S ROOM
8'9" × 8'3"

DOWN

SERVICE ELEV

TERRACE

BEDROOM
14'10" × 13'6"

CL

CL

CL

DOWN

BEDROOM
15'9" × 15'6"

CL

CL

TERRACE

MASTER BEDROOM
18'3" × 18'

CL

N NE E SE S MS W NW

WEST 81ST STREET

OPPOSITE Floor plan.
A tower apartment boasts
terraces on the first three levels.

LEFT The building's southeast
tower soars high above
Central Park.

ABOVE Emery Roth
ornamented each of the towers
with rich sculptural detail,
including festoons, composite
order columns, a broken
pediment, and a bull's-eye
window surrounded by putti
and winged mermaids.

THE TOWER

The Beresford's tower suites are among the most sought-after apartments in the city. Multileveled, they feel like miniature townhouses in the sky. This five-story apartment, renovated by Ferguson & Shamamian in 2007, features a sinuously curving stair that climbs three stories and connects the public rooms to the bedroom floors above. The building setbacks create terraces on three levels, offering spectacular views in three directions. The uppermost terrace stretches the full length of the building and is nestled between two of the building's iconic towers—one of which belongs to another apartment; it affords an unrivaled panorama of the park and the cityscape beyond. The two-story tower, an ornate dome-like structure encrusted with elaborate terra-cotta details, contains a large family room with a double-height ceiling and massive arched windows; a spiral stair accesses the gym above. Delphine Krakoff of Pamplemousse Design carried out the interior décor, creating a series of bright, lacquered spaces that feature a sophisticated mix of mid-century furnishings by some of her favorite designers, including André Arbus, Jean-Michel Frank, and Jacques Adnet, and American art, mostly from the 1906s and 1970s. The décor reinforces the light and airy quality of Roth's interior architecture.

OPPOSITE A Venini chandelier hangs from the center of the vaulted ceiling in the tower room, which is primarily furnished with white- and brown-upholstered pieces. A vintage Tobia Scarpa cocktail table sits between a pair of George Smith sofas. The arched window echoes the shape of the ceiling.

ABOVE An abstract painting by Friedel Dzubas adds rich color to the room.

OVERLEAF A new stair connecting the first three floors of the apartment gave a sense of continuity to the apartment when it was redesigned in 2007.

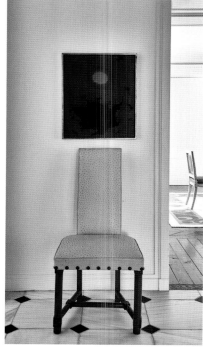

LEFT The sinuous plaster stair has a sculptural, almost abstract, quality.

ABOVE In the foyer, *Looping #2* by Adolph Gottlieb hangs above a 1950s Jacques Adnet chair.

OPPOSITE top A sycamore secretary cabinet by André Arbus, ca. 1937, which houses a gold leather drop-leaf desk top, stands in a corner of the living room.

OPPOSITE bottom A Jean Royère table occupies the center of the foyer. Friedel Dzubas's *Kronion* hangs on one of the walls.

OPPOSITE In the media room, *Rose Wide* by Kenneth Noland hangs above a sofa upholstered in an Old World Weavers fabric.

ABOVE A bright yellow Marc Newson Felt chair is evocatively juxtaposed with *Pan of Rohallion*, a bronze statue by Frederick William MacMonnies, ca. 1894.

OVERLEAF Delphine Krakoff's interiors contain a sophisticated mix of mid-century furnishings. The bright white living room is accented with pops of warm browns and blacks: the André Arbus sycamore armchairs, Al Held's painting *Phoenicia VIII*, Hervé Van der Straeten's *Branches* mirror above the Louis XIV-style mantel, the custom-made Beauvais carpet after an Arbus design, and the Art Deco baby grand piano. The custom-made kidney-shaped sofas, upholstered in a Holly Hunt fabric, add a touch of lavender to the room.

LEFT The kitchen, designed by Mark Ferguson of Ferguson & Shamamian, features a stainless-steel hood, a marble-and-granite floor, and traditional glass-fronted cabinets.

BELOW The south-facing master bedroom is decorated with drawings by Michael Canney over the fur-draped bed, a painting by Esteban Vicente, a 1930s chandelier by Carlo Scarpa for Venini, and a Diego Giacometti bench.

OPPOSITE The attic space over the tower room is used as an exercise room; its brick walls reveal the construction of the building.

OVERLEAF The uppermost terrace stretches the full length of the building and is nestled between two of the building's iconic towers, one of which belongs to another apartment.

· 10 ·
GRACIE SQUARE

I N THE LATE 1920S, EAST END AVENUE BEGAN TO EMERGE AS THE NEXT ENCLAVE FOR LUX-
ury apartments. Like Sutton Place before it, the riverfront neighborhood from 79th to 90th
Street became ripe for development. It boasted unobstructed views over the East River to
Hell Gate—the confluence of the Harlem and East Rivers—as well as the ten-acre Carl
Schurz Park, home of the newly refurbished Gracie Mansion, then the original location of
the Museum of the City of New York and later the official mayoral residence. The quiet stretch
of land, occupying the easternmost portion of the Yorkville neighborhood, had been built up with
brownstones and tenements that were primarily inhabited by German and Hungarian immigrants.
Though attempts had been made to improve the area, it was Vincent Astor's land purchase in
1927 on 86th Street between Carl Schurz Park and Avenue A and the relocation of the genteel
Miss Chapin's School to 84th Street that began to draw a stream of investors. In 1928 the Board of
Estimate approved a petition to restrict East End Avenue from 84th to 79th Street to residential use,
a motion that threw the avenue open to exclusive apartment development, relegating the coal yard
and cigar factory that had been located in the neighborhood to history. By 1929, the *New York Times*
reported that "in the Carl Schurz area an almost unbelievable transformation has been wrought
during the past two years by the replacement of tenements and small private houses with tall apartments occupying entire blocks in some instances."[1]

10 Gracie Square was the grandest of these new edifices. As buildings such as 25 East End
Avenue (1925), 520 and 530 East 86th Street (1927 and 1928, respectively) and One Gracie Square
(1928) started to go up, Eliot Cross—of Cross & Cross and Sutton Place fame—teamed with
John Drummond Kennedy and the Rhoades Kennedy Security Corporation to buy the old Italian
Hospital, which then occupied the entire riverfront from 83rd Street to Gracie Square. Incorporated
in 1905, the Italian Hospital moved to 617 East 83rd Street in 1912 but by 1928, the nondescript
six-story building represented a tremendous opportunity. In 1929
Rhoades Kennedy commissioned two firms, Van Wart & Wein
and Pennington & Lewis, to design a large, eighteen-story cooperative (with the first three of the stories below street level, fronting the river) containing forty-two apartments ranging from six
to nineteen rooms in size. By this time, Eliot Cross's name was

OPPOSITE From the arched
passageway into the living
room, Arnold Schmidt 's *Up
and Down*, 1965, by can be seen
on the far wall.

no longer linked to the project. Van Wart & Wein was well familiar with riverfront development, having worked on 439 East 51st Street (1925) and the more luxurious Campanile (1926) at 450 East 52nd Street, both in the emerging Beekman Place neighborhood. And Pennington & Lewis had just designed One East End Avenue (1928), three blocks south.

Plans replicated some of the elements of One Sutton Place, most notably a private yacht landing that in this case connected to a club space on the river—both luxuries that were obscured by the construction of the East River Drive in the late 1930s and 1940s. Like many of Candela's buildings, the interweaving of simplexes, duplexes, and—at 10 Gracie—semi-duplexes created a web of interlocking volumes and room arrangements. Van Wart & Wein designed the public rooms with ceiling heights two to four feet higher than the bedrooms—a feature that only added to the design's layered complexity. Many of the forty-two apartments, which included four maisonettes and two rooftop apartments, were custom designed, and all of them, with the exception of one six-room suite, had two or more fireplaces. Others had large bay windows overlooking the river as the building stepped back toward 83rd Street.

ABOVE The apartment house reads as three separate buildings, with a buff-colored limestone corner pavilion as its focal point.

BELOW LEFT Wilton Lloyd-Smith's twenty-room duplex penthouse included an impressive barrel-vaulted den.

BELOW RIGHT Many of the apartments had custom architectural elements, including Colley E. Williams's duplex. His living room featured elaborate pedimented bookshelves framing the fireplace.

Well aware of the building's distinctive spot, the architects were determined not to let an architectural moment slip away. Because it was perched on the edge of the park and the river, it was to be very visible from the open land below as well as from the northern section of East End Avenue and the water. As described by Harold Sterner of Pennington & Lewis, the firm that was most likely responsible for the exterior, the challenge of the job was to "provide a design sufficiently interesting for a site which might almost be said to constitute one of the corners of Manhattan Island."[2] Rising to the challenge, they designed 10 Gracie to read as three separate buildings, with the buff-colored limestone corner pavilion as the focal point, flanked by brick sections to the west and south. They continued the limestone up through the design of the water tower with a bold, elaborate screen and powerful chimney silhouettes, all of which reinforced the importance of the building.

The entrance also presented an opportunity for a distinctive, unique design. The architects extended a motor drive—once the backdrop to a 1935 *Vogue* photo shoot—through the building from Gracie Square to 83rd Street, crowning the interior concourse with a glass top. Running alongside it, a pillared gallery accessed three small vestibules and elevator banks. Stone walls, vaulted ceilings, and a Greek key frieze gave the gallery a certain elegance, while a sentry, iron gates, and the absence of a typical front door and lobby made the entrance feel discreet and undisclosed—a jewel

to be found upon approaching the building. The intimate elevator vestibules were distinguished with stylized classical details and fireplaces.

Construction continued throughout 1929 and 1930; by October 1930, the building was 35 percent sold. Early buyers included the prominent broker Frederick Martin Davies; William A. M. Burden Jr., a great-great-grandson of railroad baron Cornelius Vanderbilt; George Leary Jr., president of the Morris & Cummings Dredging Company; Douglas F. Wheeler, former head of the Wheeler-Schebler Carburetor Company; Charles V. Hickox; H. Bartow Farr; Harrison Tweed and his wife Blanche Oelrichs, a poet and playwright known by the pseudonym "Michael Strange"; and corporate lawyer Colley E. Williams. Lawyer Wilton Lloyd-Smith purchased a twenty-room duplex penthouse, and another family, undisclosed by the *New York Times*, purchased three apartments—or thirty-seven rooms—with the intent of joining them into one massive spread. Over time, residents have included critic Alexander Woollcott, Russian-born conductor Andre Kostelanetz, Gloria Vanderbilt, and Madame Chiang Kai-shek, former first lady of the Republic of China, who lived there in the 2000s until her death in 2003 at age 106.

Despite some early success, the Depression caused the building to go into foreclosure in 1937; it was sold at auction and bought by the Mutual Life Insurance Company. Today, however, 10 Gracie Square is one of the city's most celebrated cooperatives. After the East River Drive buried the first three riverfront levels, the vaunted club space was transformed into the building's own private squash court. With its impressive roofline and distinctive three-part composition, 10 Gracie still stands sentinel over the quiet and remote residential neighborhood of East End Avenue.

TOP AND ABOVE LEFT
The motor drive, topped by glass skylights, extended through the building between Gracie Square and 83rd Street. Alongside it, a pillared gallery was luxuriously appointed with stone walls, vaulted ceilings, and a Greek key frieze. The motor drive served as a backdrop for a *Vogue* photo shoot in 1935 with Jane Powell modeling a coat in front of a Cadillac.

ABOVE RIGHT Horst photographed artist and fashion designer Gloria Vanderbilt, a great-great granddaughter of Commodore Cornelius Vanderbilt, in front of a portrait of her mother in her penthouse at 10 Gracie Square, 1985.

CHAMBER
23'5" × 19'

DRESSING
ROOM

CHAMBER
18' × 13'

CL

CL

CL

MAID'S
ROOM
6'6" × 14'

MAID'S
ROOM
7' × 14'

LINEN

MAID'S
ROOM
6'6" × 14'

CL

CL

CHAMBER
15' × 16'7"

CL

CL

CL

CHAMBER
21' × 17'

CHAMBER
18' × 11'

CHAMBER
18' × 13'

CL

CL

CL

CL

MAID'S
ROOM
6' × 14'

LINEN

MAID'S
ROOM
7' × 14'

PASS.
ELEV.

CHAMBER
15' × 19'

CL

VEST.

MAID'S
ROOM
6' × 14'

CL

CL

CL

FOYER
19'4" × 17'1"

PANTRY

SERVICE
ELEV.

SERVANT'S
HALL
16'6" × 9'4"

KITCHEN
16'6" × 14'

LIBRARY
20' × 14'9"

LIVING ROOM
30' × 20'

DINING
ROOM
26' × 18'

RIVER VIEW

This twelve-room apartment, owned by the irrepressible art collector Beth Rudin DeWoody, is one of the building's semi-duplexes. The light-filled entertaining rooms have ceilings significantly higher than those in the bedrooms; a short span of steps accommodates the shifting levels. With classical interiors designed by Alan Wanzenberg for the owner in 1988, the apartment received an update in recent years at the hands of Randall Beale and Carl Lana of Beale-Lana Interior Design. They painted the walls and floors a sleek bright white and incorporated a mix of white-upholstered furniture with black accents to create an elegant yet neutral foundation for DeWoody's eclectic, ever-growing collections. This extraordinary assemblage—which changes on a rotating basis—is a far-reaching, unadulterated mix of high and low, classic and modern, traditional and contemporary. Italian and French mid-century furnishings cohabitate with antiques, bold photography, and Pop Art. Every wall is covered, including those of the gallery—the hallway leading back to the bedrooms—and every nook and cranny, including closets in some cases, reveals some sort of visual treat. The spacious, sun-filled spaces overlooking the river provide an ideal backdrop for the layers of intrigue that abound throughout the rooms.

OPPOSITE Floor plan. The B-line duplex is luxuriously appointed with four fireplaces, seven bedrooms, and six maid's rooms.

LEFT The entrance hall serves as a gallery space. On the left, Roxy Paine's sculpture *Scumak* sits beneath Sol LeWitt's *Wall Drawing #1022*, 2002, and is flanked by a pair of Gerrit Rietveld chairs. Works by Chuck Close line the wall above the stairs.

OPPOSITE David Shrigley's *Very Large Cup of Tea*, 2012, and Tom Sachs's *Balthazar Rat*, 1998, sit on the C. Bechstein piano in the living room. Next to the piano is a Ring Chair by Maria Pergay (1968). Works by Richard Artschwager, Rachel Feinstein, and Rob Wynne decorate the walls.

RIGHT Scott Covert's *Ludwig Mies van der Rohe #3*, ca. 2005, hangs above the mantel.

BELOW Three of Keith Coventry's *Estate Paintings*, 1996–97, decorate the wall above the sofa. Works by Dean Levin and Jesús Rafael Soto add pops of red. Sculptures by César, Elie Nadelman, Bosco Sodi, and Matt Johnson enliven the red-and-black coffee table.

OVERLEAF An Italian chandelier from the 1960s hangs above a custom-designed table in the dining room. Sylvester Damianos's *Blue Scape One*, ca. 1970, and Robert Wilson's video installation *Snow Owl*, 2006, add blue flourishes.

OPPOSITE TOP LEFT In a corner of the dining room, *Time Piece*, 1989, by Richard Artschwager rests on a Maria Pergay credenza. Hanging above it is a kinetic mirror by Doug Aitken entitled *The Moment Is the Moment*, 2004.

OPPOSITE TOP RIGHT In another corner of the dining room, Wyatt Kahn's *Amigo*, 2012, hangs above another Maria Pergay credenza.

OPPOSITE BOTTOM Liza Lou's *Untitled #2*, 2011–12, made entirely of woven glass beads, hangs above a Maria Pergay Drape Cabinet.

ABOVE The mantel is decorated with golden eggs by Lucio Fontana and Christo's *Wrapped New York Times, June 13, 1985*. A painting by Martin Basher hangs above, and several antique sculptures are displayed in the fireplace.

LEFT Works by E. E.
Cummings, Red Grooms, and
Jennifer Reeves decorate a wall
in the library. The bathroom
features pieces by Trey Speegle,
Jeffrey Vallance, and Alex Katz.

BELOW In the library, an
eighteenth-century copy
of a seventeenth-century
Gothic Revival Chippendale
bookcase shares the space
with works by McDermott &
McGough, Shane Ruth, and
Greg Haberny. A Tejo Remy
Rag Chair complements the
orange leather Gio Ponti sofa.

Diode Lamp (Small Green), 2006, by Marc Newson casts the media room in a green light. The custom bookcase is hung with small works of art by Judy Chicago, E. V. Day, and Adolph Gottlieb.

OPPOSITE TOP AND BOTTOM
In the master bedroom,
Alan Rath's *Watcher V*, 2005,
keeps vigil over the bed.

ABOVE Pewabic Pottery of Detroit designed the tile for the
master bathroom and Patrice Humbert of La Forge Française
created the custom metal trim. The sconces are by Tiffany, and
the artwork includes *My Footprints* by Michele Oka Doner
and *Louis Vuitton Cosmetic Case*, 2004, by Libby Black.

· 740 ·
PARK AVENUE

THE DEVELOPER JAMES T. LEE WAS A MAN OF AMBITION AND VISION; HE DID nothing half-heartedly. In March 1929 he embarked on another groundbreaking project, this one a block north of the site he and his partners had bought in 1925 and sold for a tidy profit soon thereafter. Lee, who had been living at 750 Park Avenue, convinced his neighbor the financier George S. Brewster, one of the largest shareholders of Standard Oil, to give up his Trowbridge & Livingston–designed townhouse, built just twenty years earlier, on the northwest corner of 71st Street in exchange for a suite in the new luxury cooperative that Lee was planning. Having acquired the vacated Presbyterian Hospital nurses' residence on 71st Street years earlier and an additional townhouse on Park Avenue, Lee assembled a prime corner lot on the crest on Lenox Hill. Planned and built by Lee's syndicate, the Sheldon Holding Company, construction of the limestone-clad eighteen-story building began in November, just as Straus's 720 Park was opening for residency. Lee commissioned Rosario Candela for the job but also brought on Arthur Loomis Harmon (1878–1958) as associated architect. In 1923 Lee had commissioned Harmon to design the majestic Shelton Hotel on Lexington Avenue, a massive men's hotel with club-like facilities and distinctive setbacks. The division of labor for 740 Park likely followed that of other dual-designed buildings: Candela was responsible for 740's interlocking, complex apartment configurations, while Harmon, whose firm, Shreve, Lamb & Harmon, was also involved in the design of the Empire State Building, carried out the spare, Art Deco–inspired façades. The building was completed in record time, with Lee seemingly racing against the faltering economy. By October 1930, the building's thirty apartments, ranging from nine to twenty-three rooms, were turned over to their tenant owners.

Like 720 Park Avenue, Lee's building rose to the twelfth floor in accordance with the zoning regulations that had shaped the Park Avenue street wall. But instead of having a defined cornice at that level, it fluidly ascended in a series of terraces embellished with stylized accents at the setbacks and featured striated piers running the length of the façades. The building's fluted marble base, punctuated with stainless-steel side doors that were ornamented with organic Art Deco details, added a refined yet glamorous touch. Even the characteristically withholding *New Yorker* critic T-Square, who disparaged some of Candela's other buildings, found reason to like it, writing, "Here is

OPPOSITE The stair leading up to the bedroom level features a stylized balustrade, a Beauvais runner, and hand stenciling on the curved, glazed wall.

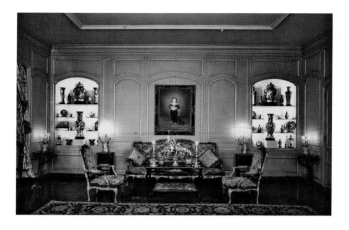

RIGHT The living room in the Rockefeller triplex included Georgian-style moldings and built-in shelves for a collection of porcelains. Francisco José de Goya y Lucientes's *The Boy in Blue*, 1791, hangs over the settee.

FAR RIGHT A portrait of John D. Rockefeller Sr. by John Singer Sargent hung in the main hall of John D. Rockefeller Jr.'s triplex.

ABOVE John D. Rockefeller Jr. (standing third from left) with his sons, Laurance (standing first from left), Winthrop (standing second from left), John (standing second from right), Nelson (front left) and David (front right), daughter, Abby (seated second from left), wife, Abby (seated fourth from left), and their respective spouses in the living room, Christmas 1947.

a pleasant, simple design, limestone throughout, with the fluted panels of the floors and the low-relief vertical and horizontal bands of the shaft ingeniously arranged. The Park Avenue entrance, trimmed with a beautiful purplish marble, is most attractive. In fact, the whole building has great dignity; one feels that thought and skill have gone into the making of it."[1]

Despite the economy, 740 Park filled quickly, with Lee's optimism buoying potential buyers. The apartments were planned expansively and offered at prices ranging from $72,000 to $215,000. The Park Avenue entrance accessed the A and B lines in the front of the building; a second entrance at 71 East 71st Street led to another lobby and the C and D lines in the western wing. Aside from three triplex maisonettes with entrances at street level, 740 consisted primarily of duplexes, with only the fourteenth and half of the seventeenth floor given over to simplexes. A long, wood-paneled hallway with travertine marble floors joined the two lobby spaces, which featured stylized stainless-steel details and grilles. Marble-floored elevator vestibules, travertine entrance galleries, curved marble staircases, multiple fireplaces, and well-equipped modern kitchens were among the amenities all tenants enjoyed. Because the apartments were sold raw, many of the owners asked Candela—or other designers—to complete their interiors.

The building had strong associations with Chase National Bank, then a relatively new financial institution that grew substantially in the 1920s under Albert H. Wiggin. The Metropolitan Life Insurance Company—whose board included Chase executives—provided the building's $4 million mortgage. Lee, also a vice president of Chase, dealt with real estate investments at the bank; for himself he chose a prime terraced duplex on the fifteenth and sixteenth floors that spanned both the C and D lines and had west-facing views of St. James Church and Central Park. His senior, Charles S. McCain, chairman of Chase, took a sixteen-room, seven-bath apartment in the front, and Lynde Selden, Albert Wiggin's son-in-law and head of the foreign department at Chase, also moved in. As part of the initial real estate transaction, Lee promised George Brewster and his wife, Eleanor, the finest apartment in the building; they claimed the second duplex on the fifteenth and sixteenth floors, consisting of twenty-three rooms that stretched the full Park Avenue width of the building and extended back along 71st Street; a mezzanine level for servants brought its floor count to three. Other early residents included a mix of blue-blooded New Yorkers such as stockbroker Bayard C. Hoppin and his brother G. Beekman Hoppin, whose family's real estate holdings included Beekman Place, successful financiers, businessmen, and scions of prominent families. Bond dealer Landon K. Thorne; Frances W. Scoville, the widow of a railroad car wheel magnate; ironworks owner Bertran H. Borden; insurance executive William Nelson Davey; Mrs. David C. Hanrahan, the great-granddaughter of Moses Taylor, the wealthiest banker of his era;

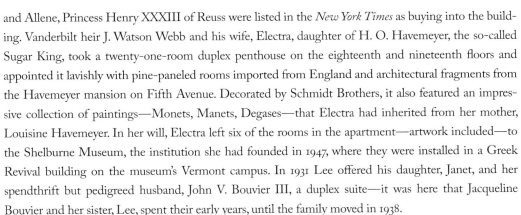

and Allene, Princess Henry XXXIII of Reuss were listed in the *New York Times* as buying into the building. Vanderbilt heir J. Watson Webb and his wife, Electra, daughter of H. O. Havemeyer, the so-called Sugar King, took a twenty-one-room duplex penthouse on the eighteenth and nineteenth floors and appointed it lavishly with pine-paneled rooms imported from England and architectural fragments from the Havemeyer mansion on Fifth Avenue. Decorated by Schmidt Brothers, it also featured an impressive collection of paintings—Monets, Manets, Degases—that Electra had inherited from her mother, Louisine Havemeyer. In her will, Electra left six of the rooms in the apartment—artwork included—to the Shelburne Museum, the institution she had founded in 1947, where they were installed in a Greek Revival building on the museum's Vermont campus. In 1931 Lee offered his daughter, Janet, and her spendthrift but pedigreed husband, John V. Bouvier III, a duplex suite—it was here that Jacqueline Bouvier and her sister, Lee, spent their early years, until the family moved in 1938.

In 1937 John D. Rockefeller Jr. purchased the Brewster apartment and commissioned Georgian specialist Mott Schmidt to update the massive suite. Though built as a cooperative, 740 became a conventional rental—as many others did—in the aftermath of the Depression, when mortgage and maintenance payments became unmanageable for many. William Zeckendorf of Webb & Knapp bought the building in 1952, only to turn around and sell it to Rockefeller months later. In 1955 Rockefeller offered up the building to the tenants—himself included—as a newly instated cooperative. In the 1950s the building continued to attract a Who's Who of New York business and society, counting R. T. Vanderbilt, Jack F. Chrysler, Mrs. Solomon R. Guggenheim, and Col. William Schiff as residents. The young and beautiful Standard Oil heiress Peggy Bancroft and her husband Tommy took over James T. Lee's apartment and threw some of the era's most elaborate parties. Society photographer Slim Aarons described her as "the hostess with the mostes'."[2] In the 1960s Sister Parish redecorated the Webb penthouse for Edgar Bronfman, head of Seagram's. Throughout its history and into the present day, 740 Park has maintained its stronghold as the city's premier address, continuing to draw some of Manhattan's most successful denizens to its sprawling and storied apartments.

TOP LEFT Peggy Bancroft in the foyer of her duplex, ca. 1958.

TOP RIGHT Electra Havemeyer Webb in her penthouse apartment with her three poodles, mid-1930s.

ABOVE The Edgar Degas painting in the living room was one of many important works of art in the Webb apartment.

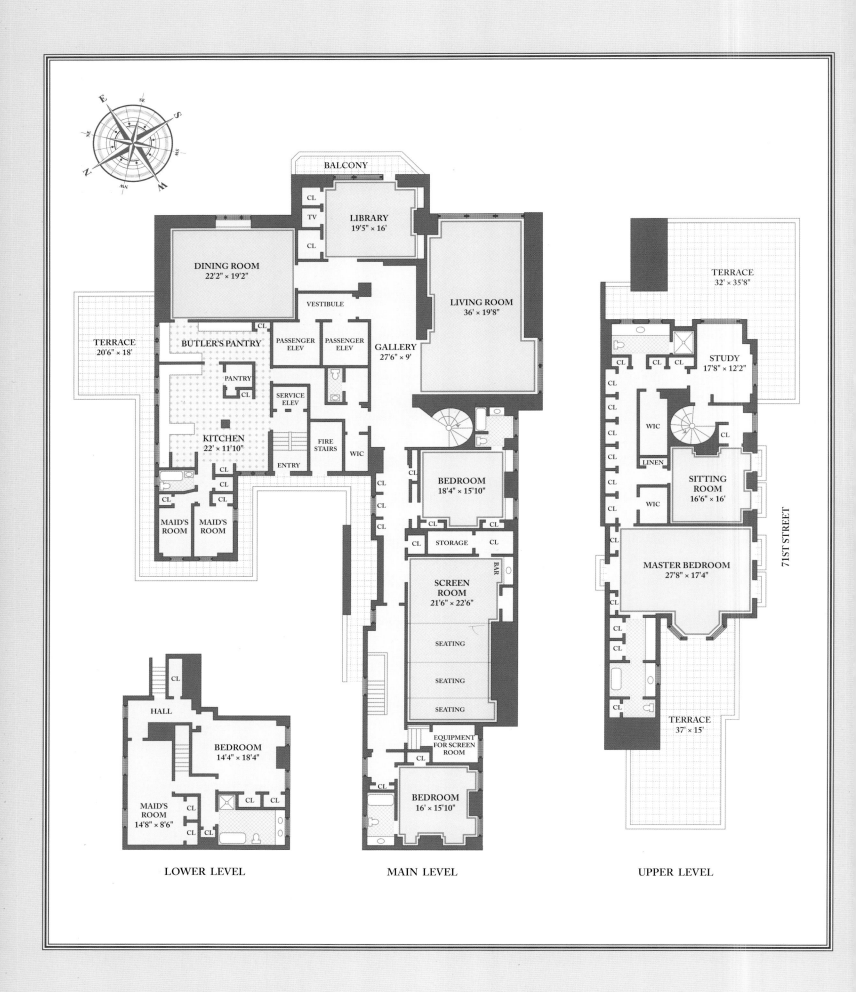

BALCONY

CL

TV

LIBRARY
19'5" × 16'

CL

DINING ROOM
22'2" × 19'2"

VESTIBULE

LIVING ROOM
36' × 19'8"

TERRACE
20'6" × 18'

BUTLER'S PANTRY

PASSENGER
ELEV

PASSENGER
ELEV

GALLERY
27'6" × 9'

PANTRY

CL

SERVICE
ELEV

KITCHEN
22' × 11'10"

FIRE
STAIRS

WIC

ENTRY

CL

BEDROOM
18'4" × 15'10"

CL

CL

CL

CL

CL

CL

MAID'S
ROOM

MAID'S
ROOM

CL

STORAGE

CL

SCREEN
ROOM
21'6" × 22'6"

BAR

SEATING

SEATING

SEATING

HALL

CL

BEDROOM
14'4" × 18'4"

MAID'S
ROOM
14'8" × 8'6"

CL

CL

CL

CL

CL

EQUIPMENT
FOR SCREEN
ROOM

CL

CL

BEDROOM
16' × 15'10"

TERRACE
32' × 35'8"

CL CL CL

STUDY
17'8" × 12'2"

CL

CL

WIC

CL

LINEN

CL

WIC

CL

SITTING
ROOM
16'6" × 16'

MASTER BEDROOM
27'8" × 17'4"

CL

CL

CL

CL

71ST STREET

TERRACE
37' × 15'

LOWER LEVEL

MAIN LEVEL

UPPER LEVEL

THE ROCKEFELLER TRADITION

Originally decorated by Bunny Williams and recently reinvigorated by Cullman & Kravis, this duplex retains much of its original character and architectural detail. The formal entrance hall is the heart of the apartment; from it, an elegant curving stair leads to the upper level, and all of the public rooms radiate off of it. A bright living room decorated in shades of pink and mint green connects to an intimate, sunlit breakfast room, complete with a window seat and an abundance of storage space masked by a cheery eighteenth-century French wallpaper. Sun streams into the expansive dining room, its walls of burgundy silk accented by wood panels inset with gilded beading. The cozy paneled library features exquisite wood details, including an intricately carved mantel and fluted pilasters with Ionic capitals. Upstairs, Cullman & Kravis chose a muted palette for the bedrooms and study. Like the many other duplexes in the building, its rooms are generously proportioned and well arranged—a Candela signature.

OPPOSITE Floor plan. The expansive apartment originally owned by J. Watson and Electra Havemeyer Webb on the eighteenth and nineteenth floors also included a mezzanine level. Edgar Bronfman occupied the apartment in the 1960s and 1970s. A subsequent owner installed the screening room.

BELOW From the foyer, double doors, set beneath a barrel vault and an architrave, lead into the library.

ABOVE The paneled library, decorated by Bunny Williams, features intricately carved original wood details, including the mantelpiece and the fluted pilasters with Ionic capitals flanking it.

OPPOSITE Eighteenth-century French wallpaper purchased from Gracie conceals storage cabinets and gives the breakfast room a cheery look.

LEFT The aqua, rose, and wine hues of the nineteenth-century Savonnerie rug, woven in the period of Louis Philippe I, coordinate with the colors of the living room.

ABOVE A black-and-gold neoclassical cabinet displays a collection of porcelain.

OVERLEAF The nineteenth-century English needlework carpet from Doris Leslie Blau complements the silk damask walls of the dining room. A Chippendale cabinet holds a collection of china.

ABOVE In the master bedroom, a custom Paley chaise covered in a Rogers & Goffigon fabric sits in front of a window that overlooks the park. Curtains in an embroidered silk fabric from Kravet coordinate with the custom bouclé finish of the walls.

OPPOSITE The delicately hand-painted doors in the dressing room were carried out in 1988. Cullman & Kravis updated the room with a new tufted ottoman in a Scalamandré fabric, a Beauvais carpet, and a Roman shade in a Cowtan & Tout fabric with a silk border.

LEFT In the foyer, Jeff Koons's *Find a Quiet Table*, 1986, and Richard Prince's *Untitled (Orange Hood)*, 1989, flank the double door leading into the dining room.

BELOW *Untitled (The Hole)*, 2007, by Piotr Uklański reflects the curve and railing of the stair leading to the upper level.

A COLLECTOR'S APARTMENT

Much has changed in this duplex since the days when the Bouvier family occupied it. In its latest incarnation, by Joe Nahem of Fox-Nahem Associates, a good deal of its architectural integrity has been preserved—the signature curving stair, the foyer, and the paneling and the moldings in some of the rooms—but the décor has an edgy, modern-day vibe, thanks to an impressive collection of contemporary art by the likes of Richard Prince, Andy Warhol, Cindy Sherman, Damien Hirst, Ed Ruscha, and Cy Twombly. At the same time, mid-century furnishings—mixed in with new custom pieces—underscore the Art Deco period in which the building was constructed. And luxurious materials such as horsehair, mink, and cashmere give the rooms a sumptuous appeal.

BELOW A seating area in the dining room includes a custom horsehair settee that matches the room's horsehair-paneled walls. Andy Warhol's *Brillo Soap Pads Box*, 1964, sits alongside, and a photographic print by Maurizio Cattelan hangs above.

OVERLEAF A cast-iron piece by Bruce Nauman entitled *Henry Moore Bound to Fail* hangs above a bolection-style mantel from Chesney's. George Condo's *Expanding Shrink Treatment*, 1986, is complemented by the dark brown of the horsehair-paneled walls.

TOP The living room walls are lacquered in a taupe brown. A series of photographic enlargements of dictionary definitions by Joseph Kosuth hang above the bar—a repurposed Damien Hirst medicine cabinet—at the end of the room.

ABOVE LEFT A pair of sofas upholstered in a Bergamo fabric flank the fireplace. John Baldessari's *Quality Material*, 1966–68, Cindy Sherman's *Untitled #96*, 1981, and Ed Ruscha's *Scream*, 1964, ornament the fireplace wall. Jules Leleu club chairs comingle with Jacques Quinet side tables.

ABOVE The living room
also features Adam McEwen's
graphite *Water Cooler*,
2011, and Robert Indiana's
Imperial Love, 1966.

LEFT In the kitchen, Warsaw-born artist Piotr Uklański spray-painted directly on the wall above a custom banquette covered in a Moore & Giles avocado leather.

ABOVE Stainless-steel cabinets and mosaic-tiled floors give the kitchen a modern appeal.

OPPOSITE A series of photographs by Robert Frank and works by Richard Prince and Mark Flood decorate the back stair.

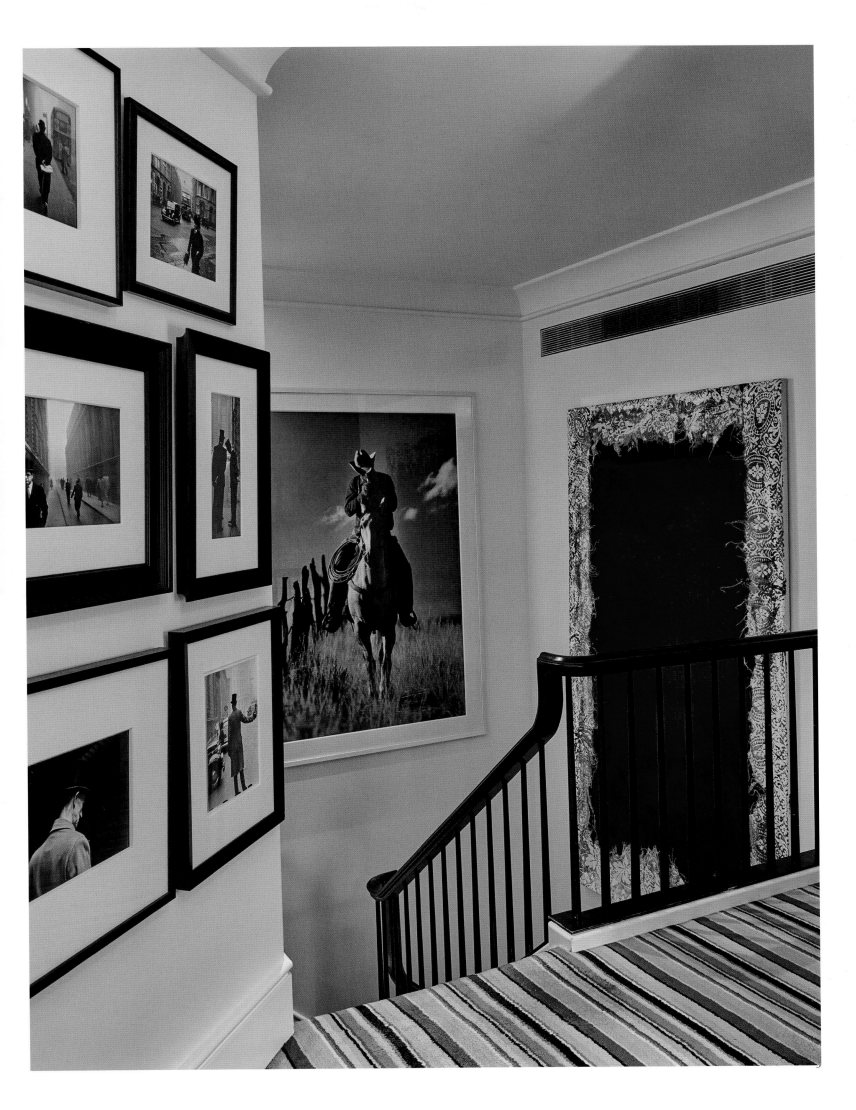

I never had a penny to my name   so I changed my name.

OPPOSITE TOP Joe Nahem stripped and limed the original millwork in the media room. The Beauvais carpet, in a David Hicks–style hexagon pattern, picks up the blues and oranges of the décor. Gregor Hildebrandt's *Today I quit life to never lose it any more*, 2013, hangs above the sofa.

OPPOSITE BOTTOM In a corner of the media room, an orange-lacquered bookcase is paired with a 1970s Pierre Paulin game table and chairs originally made for the Élysée Palace. Richard Prince's *My Name*, 1987, decorates the wall.

ABOVE The master bedroom is lined in a blush-colored cashmere. Ektacolor photographs by Richard Prince hang over the custom bed, and a Ron Gorchov painting entitled *Monsieur X*, 1979–80, hangs between the windows.

· 778 ·
PARK AVENUE

7 78 Park Avenue followed directly on the heels of 740 Park Avenue; Candela likely filed plans for the two buildings simultaneously. In May 1929, Charles Newmark, president of the Kentucky Holding Corp., announced an eighteen-story apartment on the northwest corner of 73rd Street, then known as 780 Park Avenue, just days apart from the announcement of its Candela-designed neighbor to the south, 770 Park, developed by Edgar A. Levy. Replacing the five-story Sunnyside apartment house (1889), the building—like 720 and 740 Park—represented the best of Candela's work as he continued his northern march up the avenue, transforming the thoroughfare with his distinctive brand of luxury architecture. Construction of a sophisticated neo-Georgian red brick edifice with robust limestone details and quoining ensued. It, too, rose squarely to the twelfth floor before bursting upward in an asymmetrical assemblage of setbacks, terraces, and bays. A rooftop temple masking a prosaic water tower was erected at the center, ornately festooned with limestone urns, arched openings, and Ionic columns. George Chappell, or "T-Square," the architectural critic for *The New Yorker*, opined that although the design had "more repose in the arrangement, less in detail" than 770 Park going up next door, "there [was] a distressing amount of half-baked architecture in New York, an architecture which seem[ed] to proclaim loudly a lack of the training necessary for fine work."[1] Floor plans advertised the expansive full-floor apartments with an average of sixteen rooms, a wide, thirty-six-foot-long gallery opening into an east-facing living room, and six bedrooms. With a 1930 occupancy date, R. Livingston Beeckman—the former governor of Rhode Island—purchased the duplex maisonette just as the site's excavation work was getting underway.

Although there were some early co-op sales by mid-1929, construction on the building all but stopped by July 1930, as the repercussions of the Depression began to be felt and the building frenzy of the past decade screeched to a halt. Suddenly, New Yorkers were no longer vying for such large apartments, and developers, competing with a number of equivalent buildings on the market, began to lose their shirts. By early 1931, with the interiors yet to carried out, Newmark was forced to hand over the unfinished building

OPPOSITE The gold Venetian plaster of the arched passageway between the living room and the dining room is in striking contrast to the dining room's blue-lacquered walls.

RIGHT Rosario Candela's neo-Georgian red brick building has robust limestone details. It rises squarely to the twelfth floor and then explodes upward in an asymmetrical composition of setbacks, terraces, and bays, topped by a temple that masks the water tower.

FAR RIGHT The much-talked-about wedding of actress Veronica Balfe, known on screen as Sandra Shaw, and Hollywood star Gary Cooper took place in the apartment of the bride's mother, Mrs. Paul Shields, in 1933.

to the mortgage holders. Vacant and incomplete, the building sat for nine months until a new syndicate, headed by David M. Milton, a son-in-law of John D. Rockefeller Jr., and Colonel Arthur Woods came to the rescue. In April 1931 the duo, who had successfully developed One Beekman Place, set out to complete construction and rebranded the building as 778 Park Avenue in an attempt to lure tenants with a new financial structure that included a mix of cooperatives and rentals. "The slate has been wiped clean," one real estate broker proclaimed, "excess values have been eliminated and there are not more than 7 or 8 per cent of vacancies."[2] Still, 778 Park was slow to fill; only four families were signed on by December 1931. Early residents included Thomas J. Watson, president of International Business Machines; stockbroker Colonel John W. Prentiss; Byron C. Foy, president of Chrysler's DeSoto division; Clarence C. Crispin, president of an air valve company; marine insurance broker William A. Prime; and banker W. Kingsland Macy, a future New York State senator. In 1932 Kent Cooper, the general manager of the Associated Press, purchased the duplex penthouse, which included multiple terraces and a small teahouse, and Mrs. James H. Ottley Sr. leased an eighteen-room suite. The much-talked-about wedding of actress Veronica Balfe, known on screen as Sandra Shaw, and Hollywood star Gary Cooper took place in the apartment of the bride's mother, Mrs. Paul Shields, in 1933, bringing attention to 778 Park Avenue in the press. The health of the building continued to improve as other discerning families moved in, including oil executive William Stamps Farish II and attorney John Henry Hammond, and soon its reputation was solidified. In 1959, after the death of her husband Vincent, Brooke Astor moved into a fifteenth- and sixteenth-floor duplex with four terraces and views of Central Park to the west. At that time, she asked Sister Parish to decorate, but it was Albert Hadley's décor of the library in the mid-1970s that became the apartment's showstopper. Designed to house Vincent Astor's collection of rare books, it featured brass-trimmed floor-to-ceiling bookshelves and the famous red-lacquered walls, which required ten coats of paint. Author and political commentator William F. Buckley Jr.'s maisonette—also renowned for its red library—became something of a literary salon in the 1970s and 1980s.

Brooke Astor's famous red-lacquered library was designed by
Albert Hadley in the mid-1970s to house Vincent Astor's collection of
rare books. It featured brass-trimmed, floor-to-ceiling bookshelves.

BEDROOM
20'1" × 17'9"

TERRACE

BEDROOM
26'7" × 16'8"

TERRACE

MAID'S ROOM
7'0" × 13'9"

MAID'S ROOM
8'6" × 10'6"

MAID'S ROOM
8'0" × 12'0"

CL

DRESSING ROOM

CL CL

CL CL

CL CL

CL

CL

CL

CL

CL

CL

CL CL

CL

CL

CL

CL

KITCHEN
16'9" × 10'7"

BEDROOM
12'8" × 14'2"

SERVICE EXIT

BEDROOM
10'4" × 14'6"

SERVICE HALL
11'6" × 12'7"

UTILITY

SERVICE ELEV

PASSENGER ELEV

PASSENGER ELEV

PANTRY
15'9" × 8'11"

W.I.C.
7'9" × 6'0"

BEDROOM
20'9" × 14'4"

VAULT

PRIVATE LANDING

CL

CL

CL

CL

CL

SITTING ROOM
17'6" × 13'6"

TERRACE

GALLERY
29'9" × 10'2"

DINING ROOM
19'10" × 26'0"

LIBRARY
21'7" × 17'0"

TERRACE

LIVING ROOM
28'4" × 19'2"

TERRACE

TERRACE

N NW W SW S SE E NE

PARK AVENUE PENTHOUSE

This rooftop duplex, while not the largest apartment in the building, is its most unique. With multiple terraces and a freestanding teahouse, it feels like a private house in the sky, surrounded by lush, multi-tiered gardens. The lower floor, consisting of a large living room, blue-lacquered octagonal dining room, and library, connects by a sinuous stair decorated with a mural depicting the Dance of the Seven Veils, original to the apartment, to a master suite with yet another terrace. After acquiring the apartment in 2008, its owners embarked on a two-year renovation, working with Australian architect Stephen Wang and interior designer Charles Pavarini to revive the classic space. A blend of traditional and contemporary elements, the rooms exhibit all the drama and flair for which Pavarini has become known. His theatrical lighting emphasizes the apartment's bold architectural details, lush fabrics, reflective surfaces, and furnishings—a mix of new, custom-made pieces and vintage pieces from the likes of Maison Jansen and Jean-Michel Frank. On the terraces, landscape designer Maureen Hackett introduced trees, shrubs, perennials, and seasonal flowers, creating a rooftop oasis that steps up and down around the apartment's different levels. The interior of the teahouse—a charming garden folly—evokes the ambience of Morocco with its green- and blue-tiled walls and exotic lanterns.

OPPOSITE Floor plan. Brooke Astor's apartment on the sixteenth floor was connected to a bedroom suite on the floor below.

ABOVE In the teahouse, the blue and green hand-thrown tiles, lit by great arched windows on all sides by day and lanterns by night, lend the space an exotic flair. The room is furnished with a mix of family heirlooms and flea market finds.

OVERLEAF The teahouse—the urban incarnation of a Palladian garden folly—is the pièce de résistance of the apartment. The western terrace, landscaped by Maureen Hackett, offers unrivaled views of the cityscape and Central Park.

LEFT The original owner of the apartment installed a mural depicting the Dance of the Seven Veils, ca. 1896, on the wall of the elegant curved stair.

BELOW A small bar is inset between the foyer and library.

RIGHT Four Ming dynasty tomb attendants decorate one of the shelves in the library.

BELOW The library features an original wrought-iron stair railing by Edgar Brandt, a well-known French ironworker. Interior designer Charles Pavarini covered the walls and the chairs, which he accented with bronze nailheads, in a beige Ultrasuede by Kravet.

OVERLEAF A large steel-gray velvet sofa that Pavarini designed anchors the living room, the dominant palette of which is gold and beige—from the plaster ceiling and pierced crown cove to the drapery fabric by Rubelli and the valances in a Larsen fabric, which were embroidered by Penn & Fletcher with semiprecious stones to match. An antique Maison Jansen cabinet that belonged to the owner's mother stands against the wall on the left.

TOP The color of the original stone mantel in the living room is echoed in the gold and beige palette of the décor.

ABOVE LEFT A glass-topped side table is by Lorin Marsh.

ABOVE RIGHT Pavarini customized the black leather head chairs in the dining room with dragonflies and other insects, which were embroidered by Penn & Fletcher using some of the owner's gemstones and hemp thread.

OPPOSITE A Gustavian wood chair with gilt ornamentation sits in front of a Coromandel screen.

PRECEDING PAGES In the dining room, the antique Maison Jansen dining table and console—heirlooms of the owners—are paired with side chairs by Jean-Michel Frank. A French Arts and Crafts brass screen was reconfigured to fit over mirrored cabinet doors. An antique Venini chandelier was also reconfigured for the space.

OPPOSITE The exotic wood–veneered kitchen cabinets are rimmed in stainless steel. The kitchen was designed by St. Charles.

ABOVE In the pantry, a series of mirrored doors conceal storage.

RIVER HOUSE

O N October 13, 1929, the *New York Times* announced that plans had recently been completed for a "towering cooperative" that when completed would "be one of the most imposing of the fine multi-family houses along the river area."[1] Since the early 1920s, the riverfront stretch, extending from East End Avenue to Beekman Place, had experienced a high-end transformation, and River House's two-hundred-foot-square site between 52nd and 53rd Streets, set on a bluff forty feet above the East River, was the icing on the cake. By this time, the blocks to its south had been improved with buildings such as Van Wart & Wein's Campanile, Emery Roth's Southgate, and Treanor & Fatio's Beekman Terrace Apartments. It was just a matter of time before the assembled lot—formerly occupied by the Cremo cigar factory, Consumers Brewing Company, and several tenements—sandwiched between the newly fashionable Sutton and Beekman Places, would be similarly reinvented.

The River House, Inc., headed by construction executive Leon V. Heuser, commissioned the firm of Bottomley, Wagner & White to design what would be the largest cooperative in Manhattan. The Beaux-Arts-trained William Lawrence Bottomley (1883–1951) practiced with a number of architects in New York throughout the 1920s, forming a partnership with William Sidney Wagner and A. J. White in 1928. Though he was responsible for many elegant Colonial Revival buildings and houses in Virginia and the New York environs, his best-known commission was River House. Resting on a massive base, the main portion of the building was U-shaped, rising fifteen stories around a land-scaped garden court that opened onto the river. The combination of the lot size and zoning enabled the architects to design a thin, square, ten-story tower, crowned by a curved finial, above a portion of the western leg of the U. To lend distinction to the great mass of the dark gray brick building, the architects accentuated the bay windows with vertical lines of lead-covered copper and added limestone trim. Molded window and door surrounds and terraced setbacks gave the façades an Art Deco flair. On the western side of the building, they created an elegant cobblestone entrance court for automobiles, discreetly marked by a pair of Art Deco stanchions capped with stylized eagles.

OPPOSITE In the front hall, the ceiling had to be dropped to accommodate a new cooling system. Reflective mercury-glass panels, outlined with a fluted bronze trim, were installed to visually bring back the height of the original ceiling. Antique consoles featuring deer heads pay homage to the animal motif in William Lawrence Bottomley's design for the stair rail.

ABOVE LEFT With a massive base and a thin, skyscraping tower, the main portion of the building was U-shaped, rising fifteen stories around a landscaped garden court that opened onto the river.

ABOVE CENTER The sub-grade riverfront portion of the building incorporated the rooms of River Club, as well as a private boat landing.

ABOVE RIGHT The lobby includes a wealth of stylized architectural details, lush marbles, and mirrored paintings in silver and translucent red of Mexican-inspired waterways by Jan Juta.

RIGHT The dining room of architect Archibald M. Brown, of the firm Peabody, Wilson & Brown, was stylized and spare, with Art Deco details and a bay window overlooking the river.

The building's sixty-four original apartments, offered at $35,000 to $275,000, included a mix of simplexes, duplexes, and triplexes, ranging from nine to seventeen rooms. In the northeast wing, the architects planned two lines of interlocking duplexes with varying ceiling heights on the lower floors, cleverly situating the bedroom level of one apartment over the entertaining rooms of the one below. Maids' rooms were relegated to the lower portion of the northwest wing without views; duplexes extended up the core of building, with four simplexes flanking them in the wings on each floor. The tower featured a series of large duplexes, capped by a seventeen-room penthouse triplex. Well-suited for entertaining, all of the suites featured bright, spacious rooms, some of which had large bay windows.

River House's showpiece, the lobby's evocative Art Deco gallery, extended the width of the building. It had dark stone floors and large east-facing windows that overlooked the garden and the river. Lush variegated marbles framed paintings of exotic Mexican scenes in silver and translucent red on mirrored glass by Jan Juta. Architectural details were stylized and included such elements as cornices carved with alternating star and moon motifs. Ernesta Beaux, the niece of American Impressionist Cecilia Beaux, emphasized the transcendent quality of the space with jewel-tone rugs and Biedermeier and Directoire furnishings.

With an occupancy date of October 1931, the building was slow to fill; by March of that year only 20 percent of the apartments had sold from plans. Among this early group were Marshall Field III, heir to the department store fortune; William Rhinelander Stewart, the descendant of a wealthy New York landowning family; businessman Cornelius Vanderbilt Whitney, the scion of

two prominent New York families; James A. Burden III, a great-grandson of Cornelius Vanderbilt; Ohio-based Frederick B. Patterson, president of the National Cash Register Company; mining pioneer and entrepreneur Arthur H. Bunker; and Mrs. Walter E. Maynard, the widow of a realtor, financier, and publisher. Edson Bradley Jr., president of whiskey distiller W. A. Gaines and Company, and his daughter, Julia Shipman, the widow of Bishop Herbert Shipman, shared an expansive triplex that contained several imported French rooms. Several architects also lived in the building, including the Swiss-born Maurice Fatio, architect of the Beekman Terrace Apartments, and Archibald M. Brown of Peabody, Wilson & Brown, well known for its picturesque country houses. William Lawrence Bottomley designed a curved stair railing ornamented with stylized horse figures for his own triplex. His riverfront living room included Art Deco cyma moldings around the windows, mirroring those on the façades, and an intimate oval sitting room one level down lined with murals by Ernest Peixotto.[2]

As the building was going up, a new club "embrac[ing] features of certain well-known London clubs" was announced.[3] Located in the southern wing of the building, with two sublevels incorporated into the riverfront bluff, River Club—as it was known—was promoted as an athletic and social club; it quickly drew the interest of society. Originally presided over by Kermit Roosevelt, a son of Theodore Roosevelt, it had six hundred members, two hundred of whom were out-of-

towners, and counted Astors, Vanderbilts, Webbs, Pratts, and Fields among its ranks. In addition to twenty-six guest suites, the club had two tennis courts, a swimming pool, a lounge, and—before the intrusion of the FDR Drive—a private boat landing on the lowest level for members "addicted to their yachts." Designed by Bottomley, Wagner & White and Ernesta Beaux, the sports facilities and adjacent lounge had a country club atmosphere, while the grill and oyster bar above were decorated in shades of black and red, echoing the more sophisticated scheme of the lobby. Wallpaper depicting sea battle scenes from the American Revolution, painted by Italian artist D. C. Sindona, graced the dining room walls. A living room, one level up, featured an elegant Chinese bird-and-flower wallcovering. Enthusiastically described by one critic as "a sparkling sapphire set in platinum," the ballroom was the club's glamorous centerpiece, decorated with silver-leafed wallpaper, sapphire glass panels on the pilasters and ceiling, and three-tiered Murano-glass chandeliers.[4]

Despite the popularity of the club, apartments still sat vacant and by March 1932, the building fell into receivership. River Club lost possession of its quarters—leasing its rooms instead—and rentals began to be offered at the cost of the maintenance fee with an option to buy after four years. Though this incentive drew additional residents, including stockbroker Robert D. Pruyn, lawyer Preston Davie, and railroad and business executive William R. Coe, among others, the financial health of the building was slow to recover, like that of many others designed and built on the brink of the Depression. Eighty years later it stands as one of Manhattan's most atmospheric and ambitious apartment buildings, perching majestically on the edge of the water at the end of a quiet cul-de-sac and anchored by the elegant River Club.

TOP LEFT River Club's ballroom was decorated with silver-leafed wallpaper, sapphire glass panels, and fountain-like Murano-glass chandeliers.

TOP RIGHT The Art Deco character of River House carried through even to River Club's swimming pool lounge, with its stylized stepped openings.

ABOVE LEFT An oval sitting room in William Lawrence Bottomley's triplex was lined with murals by Ernest Peixotto.

ABOVE RIGHT Bottomley's brass stair railing featured stylized wrought-iron figures of horses.

UPPER FLOOR

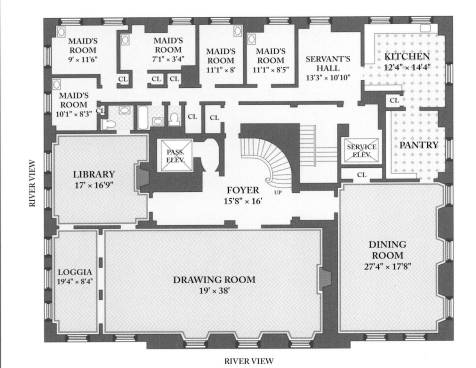

LOWER FLOOR

AMERICAN ART DECO

This storied and glamorous triplex exudes the style and panache that infuses much of Bottomley's 1930s design for the building. Once the apartment of the architect and his wife, Harriet, the rooms retain many of their exquisite original details, including his stylized stair railing, moldings, and paneling. The fact that architect I. M. Pei's wedding took place in the living room in 1942 only adds to the apartment's luster—the Bottomleys offered the space to Pei's fiancée, Eileen Loo, a friend of their daughter's. In more recent years, William Sofield of Studio Sofield overhauled the suite, honoring Bottomley's design but also injecting that extra oomph to give the rooms a sumptuousness that exceeds its previous incarnation. Staying true to the Art Deco style of the building, he introduced new wrought-iron grilles that echo the stylized motifs in the lobby to conceal modern air-conditioning vents. And, to give the décor a cosmopolitan edge harking back to the sophisticated splendor of New York in the 1920s, he covered walls in lacquer, embossed leather, mirrors, and hand-painted paper. Mid-century furniture from Maison Jansen, James Mont, and the like comingle with custom Sofield pieces in a succession of comfortable yet incredibly chic interiors with prime views of the East River.

OPPOSITE Floor plan. The duplex tower apartments at River House enjoy views in all four directions. In addition to the requisite entertaining rooms—including a loggia— they have an ample kitchen wing and seven bedrooms upstairs.

BELOW An elegant curved stair spans the three floors of the apartment. Sofield restored and extended Bottomley's stair rail. The stair runner was woven as one continuous piece on an antique tapestry loom.

OVERLEAF In the living room, the original paneling was conserved and refinished with an ivory waxed paint. Furnishings include an armchair and sofa by Maison Jansen and antique Japanese pieces, as well as a pair of vintage bergères by Paul Follot upholstered in a hand-woven silk. Lucien Freud's etching *Pluto Aged 12* rests on the mantel.

In the dining room seating area, a pyrite lamp sits on an antique sycamore drum table. The custom swivel chair is upholstered in an ivory silk moiré with silk fringe. The floors are mahogany with an ebony stain.

RIGHT The seating area also includes a custom lilac leather sofa paired with a vintage Max Kuehne coffee table of wood and silver leaf. To conceal a wall-mounted television, Nancy Lorenz was commissioned to create panels in highly burnished silver leaf that slide on a custom track. A Michele Oka Doner sculpture of metal and gold leaf is featured on the sycamore console table.

BELOW Adaptable to various entertaining configurations, the dining room has a functional chef's range and a pair of amethyst marble-topped bar tables for casual use. When necessary, the bar tables can be separated and placed against the wall to serve as consoles, allowing the dining table to expand to seat twenty. The ivory velvet chair backs are embroidered with Roman numerals to facilitate placed seating.

ABOVE A 1930s Maison Jansen chandelier hangs in the vestibule that leads to the salon on the first level of the triplex.

RIGHT The walls in the oval salon are covered in gauffered leather panels. A silk brocade curtain was woven to complement the walls; when opened, it reveals a television. The chandelier is from Nancy Reagan's White House. A custom bronze fire screen is fitted with fluted rose-colored glass. Concealed doors lead to a powder room with blood orange waxed-plaster walls and a full bar/wine room with walls lacquered in a vivid moss green.

ABOVE The octagonal-shaped kitchen has steel-and-glass cabinetry and Belgian black marble countertops. A pair of vintage opaline-glass lanterns by Seguso hangs above the island.

ABOVE LEFT The cloakroom walls are covered in a crackled black-enameled canvas. A Maison Jansen Empire-style chair pulls up to a 1920s dressing table by Robert Pansart.

ABOVE RIGHT A tiny reading room, tucked in next to the stair, has a balcony overlooking it. The walls are finished in a hand-rubbed black lacquer. A Soane desk with a waxed-leather top is paired with a vintage Ole Wanscher desk chair.

OPPOSITE Flanking the bed in the master bedroom is a pair of James Mont chinoiserie nightstands.

RIGHT A custom beechwood and gilt Louis XVI-style bed has a hand-embroidered silk headboard with a motif inspired by Armand-Albert Rateau. A suite of French parchment screens by Maison Dominique, ca. 1940, stands behind the bed.

BELOW In the master bathroom, the vanity drawer fronts are made of glass panels inset with antique lace. The tub and basin fittings, by P. E. Guerin, have an antique gold finish and rock crystal handles. De Gournay's hand-painted Fishes in Blue Pearl wallcovering lines the toilet room.

· 834 ·
FIFTH AVENUE

ONE YEAR AFTER THE SUCCESS OF 960 FIFTH AVENUE, DEVELOPER ANTHONY Campagna set out to surpass himself with plans for a luxurious apartment hotel on Fifth Avenue between 64th and 65th Streets. In April 1929 the *New York Times* announced the sale of four mid-block mansions—the houses of Aimee Guggenheim, Frank Jay Gould, Frederick Lewisohn, and the Bovee School—that together occupied a 120-foot span along the park. Again, Campagna—who had actually acquired the sites over a two-year period—called upon Rosario Candela to produce designs for a new thirty-six-story apartment hotel cooperative that was to be one of the tallest buildings on Fifth Avenue north of 57th Street. Though the market crash did not halt Campagna's grand plans, the building became simply a cooperative—its hotel component was dropped—and its height was reduced. Later that year, construction began on a sixteen-story symmetrical limestone building set back on the upper floors, creating several stories of cascading terraces overlooking the park. When the corner holdout house—a Beaux-Arts mansion belonging to Mrs. James B. Haggin—became available in 1930 after Candela's building was well underway, Campagna asked Cross & Cross, who had just worked on 960 Fifth Avenue, to file plans for an addition to extend the building to the corner of 64th Street— or another twenty feet. Though virtually indistinguishable from Candela's earlier design, the addition stretched Candela's otherwise symmetrical Fifth Avenue façade another three bays.

The original portion of the building contained mainly simplexes, but the annexed southern section—or A line—consisted primarily of duplexes. Like 960 Fifth Avenue, it manifested Candela's ability to combine simplexes, duplexes, and one penthouse triplex into a complex puzzle of floors and plans while maintaining an understated, classic, and almost deceptively simple limestone façade. Completed in 1931, 834 Fifth Avenue culminated the successful Candela–Cross & Cross partnership in what was—and still is—considered one of New York's most magnificent cooperatives. As an extra selling point to draw tenants in the increasingly competitive field of apartment design, a 2,000-square-foot garden designed by the renowned landscape architect Ferruccio Vitale was added to the rear, creating a private oasis for the building's residents.

OPPOSITE One of a pair of ceramic owls, bought from a dealer in Paris, and a lantern, formerly in Jayne Wrightsman's house in Palm Beach, adorn the early nineteenth-century ironstone mantel in the winter garden.

Despite the bleak financial climate in 1931, the building opened for occupancy on October 1 with the majority of the twenty-four grand apartments sold. Banker Hugh B. Baker, then president of the National City Company, secured the expansive triplex penthouse. In addition to a sweeping stair connecting all three levels, the twenty-four-room penthouse included a thirty-three-foot-long living room, a twenty-seven-foot-long dining room, an atmospheric solarium, and multiple terraces. Cincinnati native Carl J. Schmidlapp, vice president of the Chase National Bank, purchased a twenty-four-room duplex suite for $275,000, all cash. Even Margaret Haggin, the young widow of mining magnate James Haggin, embraced apartment living after selling her townhouse. She did not have to move far to establish herself in her new duplex at 834 Fifth Avenue. Other early residents included Mrs. Elden C. DeWitt, widow of the founder of E. C. DeWitt, a medicine company; Ezra D. Bushnell, director of the Hamilton Trust; Mrs. William A. M. Burden, granddaughter of William H. Vanderbilt; engineer Ray P. Stevens, the president of many railroad and electric companies; Mrs. John E. Berwind, widow of one of the largest coal operators in the country; banker Henry Graves, who funded the Patek Philippe Henry Graves Supercomplication watch; and Dr. James F. McKernon, former president of the New York Post-Graduate Medical School and Hospital. In the 1940s and 1950s Elizabeth Arden (née Florence Nightingale Graham) resided in the southern penthouse in a stylish aerie decorated in part by Russian designer Nicolai Remisoff. In 1946 Laurance S. Rockefeller, a grandson of John D. Rockefeller Sr., purchased the building after its shareholders lost it to foreclosure in the mid-1930s. He took over the Baker apartment, commissioning Harrison & Abramowitz to renovate. After Rockefeller's death in 2004, Rupert Murdoch, owner of the News Corporation, purchased and renovated this iconic suite.

OPPOSITE In the 1940s and 1950s, cosmetics entrepreneur Elizabeth Arden resided in the southern penthouse.

ABOVE, CLOCKWISE FROM TOP LEFT Banker Hugh B. Baker's expansive triplex penthouse featured a solarium; a dining room with a molded ceiling; a sweeping stair connecting all three levels; and a living room with a wood-beamed ceiling.

OVERLEAF Floor plan. The building's triplex penthouse featured a curved stair that connected the three levels, generous entertaining spaces on the second level, and multiple terraces. Originally owned by banker Hugh B. Baker, it later belonged to Laurance S. Rockefeller.

14TH FLOOR

STAFF ROOM

STAFF ROOM

STAFF ROOM

CL

STAFF ROOM

STAFF ROOM

CL

CL

CL

CL

SERVICE ELEV.

DOWN

UP.

PASS. ELEV.

PASS. ELEV.

VESTIBULE

WIC

CL

CL

SITTING ROOM
16' × 16'

CL

CL

UP

GUEST ROOM
14'6" × 19'6"

GALLERY

UP

DOWN

CL

GALLERY
19'6" × 10'6'

CL

CL

CL

CL

CL

CL

MASTER BEDROOM
19'6" × 17'

CL

CL

CL

CL

CL

UP

STUDY
18' × 16'

DRESSING ROOM

BEDROOM
21' × 14'6"

OFFICE
12'6" × 9'

BEDROOM
12'6" × 14'

FIFTH AVENUE

16TH FLOOR

SERVICE ELEV.

PASS. ELEV.

PASS. ELEV.

UP

TERRACE

LIBRARY
19'6" × 19'

TERRACE

DOWN

STUDIO
19'6" × 19'

TERRACE

15TH FLOOR

DOWN   UP

SERVICE ELEV.

PASS. ELEV.

PASS. ELEV.

BAR

CL

STAFF
DINING ROOM
14' × 19'6"

KITCHEN
21' × 24'6"

PANTRY

CL   CL

SITTING ROOM
12'6" × 13'

ENTRY FOYER

DOWN

CL

GALLERY
19'6" × 14'

LIVING ROOM
21' × 32'

CL

DOWN

DINING ROOM
21' × 24'

CL

CL

TERRACE

HENRI SAMUEL IN NEW YORK

The palatial Carl J. Schmidlapp duplex is one of the largest original apartments on Fifth Avenue. In 1984 its owners, Susan and John Gutfreund—who loved to entertain—enlisted architect Thierry Despont and legendary French designer Henri Samuel to reconfigure and decorate the suite. At the heart of the apartment lies a great square gallery and stair hall that links the public rooms on the lower floor—a dining room and winter garden—to a forty-foot-long living room above, created by removing some walls, with five windows overlooking the park. A series of bedrooms extend along 64th Street on the lower level; the kitchen and an extensive web of servants' halls, pantries, and staff rooms meander to the northeast in the back of the building. Upstairs, in addition to the living room, are a smoking room and the large master suite, complete with a dressing room, sitting room, and large original Art Deco bathroom. Samuel's rooms stand as a testament to the late decorator's genius and groundbreaking eclectic style. In the 1970s and 1980s, his work was de rigueur, and the impressive client list he accumulated included Vanderbilts, Rothschilds, and royalty. An alumnus of the vaunted Maison Jansen, Samuel revolutionized the world of interior design with his exotic assemblages of old and new—a novel concept at the time—and his uncanny ability to capture the spirit of the place and his clients—in this case, an ardent admirer of France. At 834 Fifth Avenue, Samuel's work includes the enchanting winter garden with its hand-painted coffered ceiling. He designed the room around a set of antique Chinese panels that the Gutfreunds had previously purchased. All the rooms are filled with wonderful pieces, including English, French, and Russian antique furnishings and beautiful *objets*. Susan Gutfreund, a decorator in her own right, found many of the pieces, each of which has a fascinating history and provenance; the winter garden, for example, is furnished with chairs from a Danish palace, a Russian Bessarabian rug from a Belgian château, and an early nineteenth-century ironstone mantelpiece. Exquisitely appointed and brimming with inspirations drawn from a wide range of sources, the apartment has timeless and classic appeal.

OPPOSITE TOP The design of the entrance and stair hall, carried out by Thierry Despont, incorporates painted door panels purchased from Henri Samuel. The Empire console, flanked by a pair of nineteenth-century Russian chairs, is paired with a nineteenth-century mirror from Denmark. Beneath the console is a bronze sculpture of a racehorse.

OPPOSITE BOTTOM The walls of the stair hall simulate the effect of rustication, giving the large double-height space a powerful architectural presence. A Russian chandelier hangs at center, and an eighteenth-century French screen, shot through with silver thread, unfolds beneath the stair.

ABOVE In the winter garden, a side table that was formerly in Jayne Wrightsman's Palm Beach house is decorated with coral candlesticks from Trapani, Sicily.

OVERLEAF Henri Samuel designed the color scheme and décor of the winter garden around a set of eighteenth-century Chinese panels, originally from a château in Belgium, that the Gutfreunds had already purchased. Samuel incorporated the panels into the architecture of the room, which was hand painted by the Atelier Mériguet-Carrère. A Diego Giacometti coffee table stands atop a Russian Bessarabian rug from a château in Belgium. The chairs, originally from a palace in Denmark, were reupholstered by Gael de Brousse.

PRECEDING PAGES Originally from Parham Park in England, the Robert Adam furniture in the dining room, including three consoles, are from Jayne Wrightsman's collection. An eighteenth-century French chandelier hangs above a reproduction Adam table and Sir John Soane–designed carpet. Samuel reproduced the striped fabric for the wall panels and draperies from an eighteenth-century textile; the pink under-curtain fabric was a gift from Karl Lagerfeld.

ABOVE In the center of the upstairs landing is an Empire table stacked with art and design books. Obelisks purchased from a dealer in Paris flank the entrance into the living room, the doors of which were gilded by the same company that re-gilded the torch of the Statue of Liberty during its restoration.

LEFT A Russian urn-shaped clock on the upstairs landing was found at Steinitz Antiques in Paris.

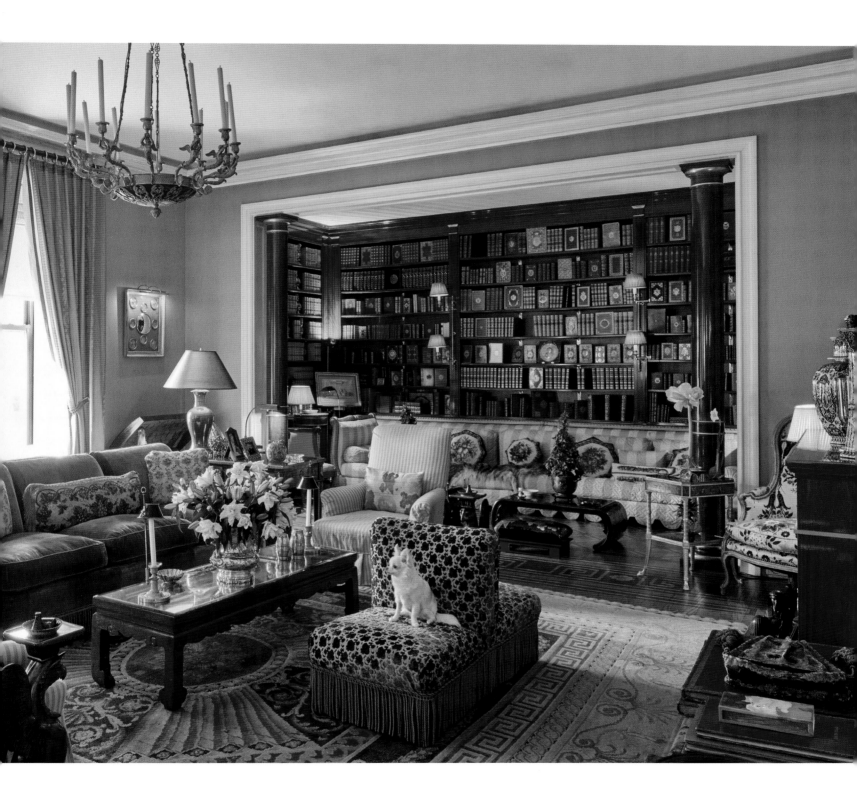

ABOVE A library niche—an idea suggested by Jayne Wrightsman based on a similar design element in the Duke and Duchess of Windsor's house in Paris—breaks up the length of the living room. Fronting the niche is a long yellow-and-white striped sofa that once belonged to Hubert de Givenchy. The eighteenth-century carpet was designed by Robert Adam for Syon House in London.

OVERLEAF The walls of the upstairs smoking room are covered with seventeenth-century leather panels; an eighteenth-century Swedish painting hangs above the sofa, flanked by bookcases from Steinitz. A clock from the collection of Hubert de Givenchy sits atop the bookshelf between the windows. Silver Russian cigar boxes—part of John Gutfreund's collection—adorn the coffee table.

OPPOSITE An upstairs sitting room features an eighteenth-century painted trumeau mirror and a collection of porcelain silhouettes of the Danish royal family. A Diego Giacometti coffee table, comfortable seating, and a needlepoint rug round out the décor.

ABOVE A bed designed by Samuel stands against walls covered in raw silk woven in a crosshatch pattern. The taffeta chiné and green hand-painted trim of the corona were inspired by Madame de Pompadour's bed hangings at the Château de Bellevue, built in 1750; the embroidered coverlet is an exact copy of a textile made by Madame Delaney, a famous eighteenth-century embroiderer.

OPPOSITE In the guest room, Henri Samuel reproduced an antique silk fabric in a heavy cotton, using it for the canopy of the bed he designed as well as for the bedcovers, upholstery, and walls. The Chinese embroidered-silk screen was purchased at a manor house sale in Scandinavia.

ABOVE The décor of this bedroom is based on Napoleon's blue-and-white-striped battlefield campaign tent, carried out in fabric from Le Manach.

OVERLEAF The kitchen still features its original cabinets, which the Gutfreunds simply repainted. To organize placement of the many services that are stored inside, a photographic system was adopted.

· 173 AND 176 ·
PERRY STREET

THROUGHOUT THE FIRST DECADES OF THE TWENTIETH CENTURY, WHILE MUCH OF Manhattan's residential cityscape was being transformed, the industrial waterfront stretching along the Hudson River just west of Greenwich Village sat untouched. A hodgepodge of brick walk-ups, tenements, and low-rise warehouses, the area fronted a series of working piers and docks. During the period when New York's commerce and travel revolved around shipping, the Hudson River waterfront was a major entry point into the city. The Chelsea Piers, a continuous ornamental bulkhead designed by Warren & Wetmore in 1910 that extended from West 23rd Street to Little West 12th Street, was the city's premier passenger ship terminal, serving the Cunard Line. Just to the south, facing West Street in the vicinity of Perry Street, were the more utilitarian piers of the Quebec Steamship Co., the Southern Pacific Steamship Co., and various freight docks. The elevated West Side Highway, built between 1929 and 1951, effectively cut the river off from the streets of lower Manhattan; even though the highway was shut down in the 1970s, it was not completely demolished until the late 1980s. The last of the Chelsea Piers were dismantled in 1991.

Thus, it was not until the late 1990s that developers began to tap into the potential of the far West Side, a move that coincided with the reconfiguration of Westway—a failed 1970s and 1980s attempt to bury the West Side Highway—into Hudson River Park. Richard Meier's pair of sleek, minimalist glass towers at 173 and 176 Perry Street marked a sea change. At the time of their completion in 2002, the two pristine buildings signaled the end of the area's blighted past, almost singlehandedly making this distant precinct of the city popular overnight. The artistic set that once populated buildings like the Beresford started to migrate downtown as a new type of building—much like an apartment version of Philip Johnson's Glass House—began to redefine the concept of luxury living.

OPPOSITE The wood-lined entrance hall, decorated with a driftwood bench and a large, black Anish Kapoor sculpture against the far wall, serves as a foil to the apartment's bright, open living space.

With Richard Meier's scheme—which took all of twenty minutes to sketch out—the idea of the "starchitect"-designed apartment building was relaunched (Candela could be considered the starchitect apartment designer of the 1920s). Born and raised across the river in New Jersey, Meier achieved international fame with buildings such as the Barcelona Museum of Contemporary Art and the Getty Center in Los Angeles. A modernist, he is considered one of the New York Five, along with his second cousin Peter

Eisenman, Michael Graves, Charles Gwathmey, and John Hejduk, and his practice, founded in 1963, is based in New York. In addition to winning the prestigious Pritzker Prize in 1984, he was awarded the AIA Gold Medal in 1997. But, despite having designed modernist glass buildings inspired by the work of the mid-century modernists, particularly Le Corbusier, all over the world, Meier had yet to design a building from the ground up in Manhattan; his 1968 conversion of the Bell Telephone Laboratory into Westbeth, a complex of affordable apartments and studios for artists two blocks north of Perry Street, was his largest commission in the city to date.

For the Perry Street Apartments, Meier partnered with Charles Blaichman, Richard Born, and Ira Drukier to purchase the sites on West Street for $12 million. Meier's plan, which originally included a hotel on the site of the Perry Street garage, detailed two fifteen-story towers with expansive glass curtain walls flanking Perry Street—a cobblestoned street of low-rise buildings reminiscent of Old New York. Both buildings featured one apartment per floor and floor-to-ceiling exposures in four directions. In the larger of the two, the south tower (176 Perry), each unit measured 4,000 square feet, whereas in the smaller north tower (173 Perry), the units were half the size. All twenty-eight units were sold as raw space for $2,000 a square foot and could be finished either by Meier's office or by a designer of the owner's choice.

ABOVE Richard Meier's pair of apartment buildings flank Perry Street; the Empire State Building can be seen between them in the distance. His third tower, just to the right on Charles Street, continues the same crystalline aesthetic. It was completed in 2006.

BELOW Jean-Georges Vongerichten's restaurant Perry St, which opened in 2005 in the ground floor of 176 Perry Street, was designed by Thomas Juul-Hansen in an elegant minimalist style.

OPPOSITE Floor plan. Three floors at 176 Perry Street were combined into one swank apartment with three bedrooms, a double-height living room, and an expansive master suite.

New York had yet to see apartment buildings with such expansive curtain walls. And, as is the case with most modern architecture, every minute detail needed to be thoroughly exacting, making the buildings expensive and tricky to construct. But with Richard Meier headlining the project and the buildings' crisp, innovative lines and bright, sun-filled rooms, their appeal was unprecedented. A number of celebrities, actors, artists, and designers, including Calvin Klein, Martha Stewart, Hugh Jackman, and Nicole Kidman, were lured by the clean minimalism of the spaces and the river views. Jean-Georges Vongerichten's swank restaurant Perry St opened in 2005 on the ground floor of 176 Perry Street, giving the towers even greater cachet.

In 2002 the concept of the starchitect-designed building was novel and fresh. The Perry Street Apartments ushered in a new phase of luxury living in New York, paving the way for buildings by the likes of Zaha Hadid, Bjarke Ingels, Tadao Ando, and Frank Gehry, both downtown and on the now-thriving Hudson River waterfront.

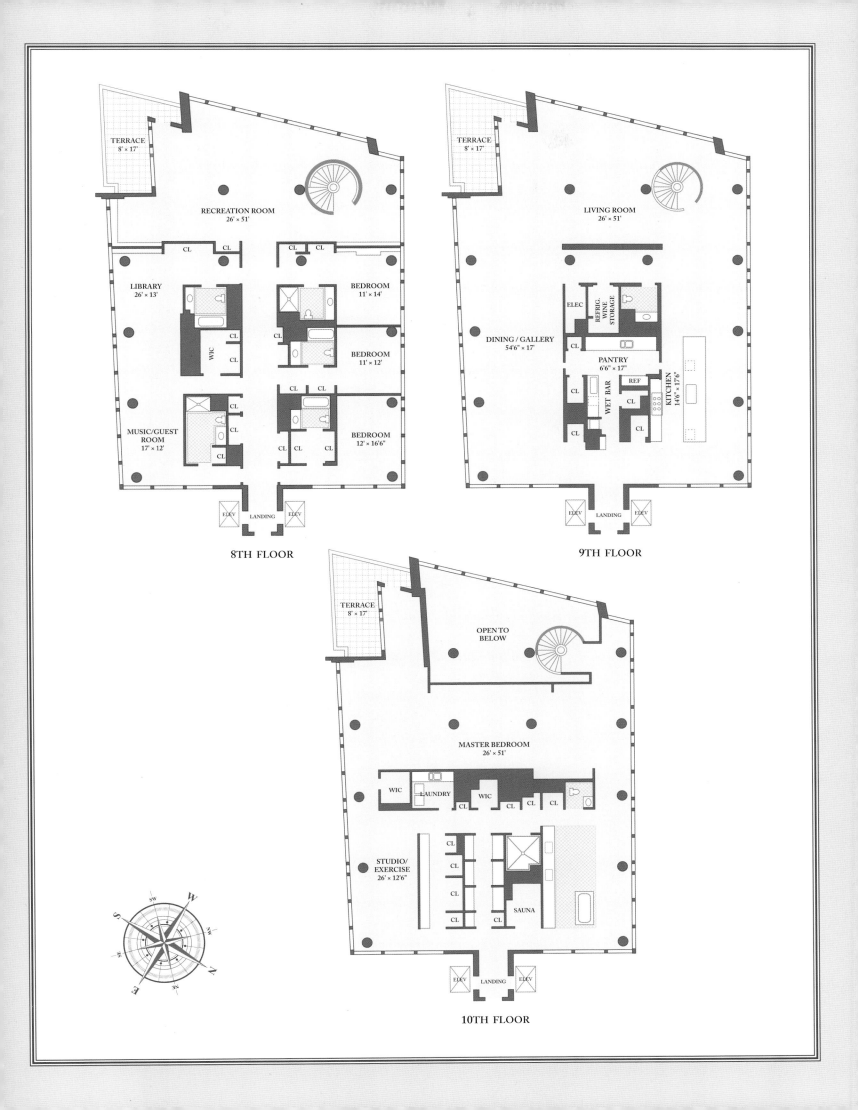

8TH FLOOR

TERRACE
8' × 17'

RECREATION ROOM
26' × 51'

CL CL   CL CL

LIBRARY
26' × 13'

BEDROOM
11' × 14'

WIC

CL

BEDROOM
11' × 12'

CL

CL CL

MUSIC/GUEST
ROOM
17' × 12'

CL
CL
CL

CL

BEDROOM
12' × 16'6"

CL CL CL

ELEV   LANDING   ELEV

9TH FLOOR

TERRACE
8' × 17'

LIVING ROOM
26' × 51'

ELEC   REFRIG.   WINE   STORAGE

CL

DINING / GALLERY
54'6" × 17'

PANTRY
6'6" × 17'

CL

WET BAR

REF

CL

KITCHEN
14'6" × 17'6"

CL

ELEV   LANDING   ELEV

10TH FLOOR

TERRACE
8' × 17'

OPEN TO
BELOW

MASTER BEDROOM
26' × 51'

WIC   LAUNDRY   WIC   CL   CL CL CL

STUDIO/
EXERCISE
26' × 12'6"

CL
CL
CL
CL

CL

CL

SAUNA

ELEV   LANDING   ELEV

PERRY STREET MODERNE

The Canadian design duo of George Yabu and Glenn Pushelberg transformed their raw space into a stylish sanctuary abounding in art and interest. The couple, well known for their award-winning hotels, stores, and restaurants, carved out smaller, more intimate spaces in the open plan for the bedrooms and designed an enclosed, wood-lined entrance sequence to counterbalance the large, open living and dining space. The muted palette and the floor-to-ceiling windows create a backdrop for their eclectic and uplifting collections of whimsical artifacts, furnishings, and art.

In the living room, a Gabetti Isola rug lies between a 1970s French rocking chair and Roberto Sebastian Matta's *Sacco Alato*, 1971.

ABOVE Two John Widdicomb chairs flank a carved Indian side table from Odegard in front of the view of the Hudson River Park.

OVERLEAF The open living space, which features the building's cylindrical concrete columns, is divided into living and dining sections. Sheer curtains let the street views in but provide privacy.

OPPOSITE TOP LEFT Three busts by the Gao Brothers sit atop a vintage sideboard.

OPPOSITE TOP RIGHT A Kohei Nawa *PixCell-Deer* is covered in artificial crystal glass beads.

OPPOSITE BOTTOM An Yves Klein 1963 Table Bleue sits in front a large, custom-made Yabu Pushelberg sofa. Behind it, Gio Ponti chairs frame Shao Fan's painting *Two Pines*.

ABOVE A Philippe Jean screen stands behind a glass table that is paired with 1950s Brazilian senate chairs and a floor lamp from Esempi del '900. A Dumbacher Brothers sculpture decorates the wall.

OPPOSITE Solid wood stools contrast with the sleek minimalism of the kitchen.

ABOVE An assortment of decanters, bowls, teapots, and fanciful objects decorate the glass shelves that hang in front of the kitchen's large windows.

OVERLEAF A guest room includes a plush chair from ABC Carpet & Home, a vintage Warren Platner sofa from Knoll International, and a series of artistically arranged drawings by Santiago Rubino.

OPPOSITE TOP The media room, carried out by Louis Interiors in Toronto, is entirely cushioned in purple. The lighting includes a pair of Zanotta sconces and an Angelo Lelli Cobra Light Sculpture table lamp.

OPPOSITE BOTTOM Yabu and Pushelberg designed the master bathroom in travertine.

RIGHT They designed the dressing room to feel intimate and enclosed. A Joaquim Tenreiro chair stands in front of one of the building's structural columns.

OVERLEAF The master bedroom is appointed with a Casamilano bed, vintage benches, a chair from Arquitetura e Decoração in Rio de Janeiro, and Paavo Tynell adjustable ceiling light fixtures.

PRINCELY RAJASTHAN

Miami Interiors

VANITY FAIR PORTRAITS

· 15 ·
CENTRAL PARK WEST

COLUMBUS CIRCLE, AT THE BASE OF CENTRAL PARK WEST, WAS LONG CONSIDERED A natural locus of development as Manhattan's march uptown proceeded apace. Laid out as the Grand Circle in Frederick Law Olmsted's plan for Central Park in 1869, it represented one of the park's great entryways, but it never achieved the same level of prestige as its eastern counterpart. Its identity was more transient; it was once an outdoor concert space, then a theater location, and later part of a strip of automobile dealers. In the 1920s and 1930s, Columbus Circle became the anchor of the line of new upscale brick-and-stone apartment houses and hotels transforming Central Park West. Harperley Hall, the first cooperative on the thoroughfare at 64th Street, opened in 1911. Sixteen years later, the Mayflower and the Plymouth Hotels, both designed by Emery Roth, architect of the Beresford and other Central Park West landmarks, began to rise between 61st and 62nd Streets. Each of the Renaissance Revival buildings covered half of the block front and was distinguished by a different water tower. Later joined through the lobby, the two hotels became one, simply known as the Mayflower. Though not one of Roth's masterpieces, it was comfortable and unpretentious. What it lacked in distinction, it made up for with its prime location and superlative views.

By 2004, the Mayflower's glory days were long past, and much of its façade's terra-cotta detail had been stripped. Backing up to a vacant lot running along Broadway, it was a holdout among glitzier newcomers, including the Trump International Hotel & Tower next door and the Time Warner Center across Columbus Circle. But its owners—the Goulandris family, represented by John J. Avlon—having assembled the site as far back as the 1970s, had a plan. In 2004 they commanded the highest price paid for land in Manhattan to date, making it the most expensive site in the city. The developers, Arthur and William Lie Zeckendorf, grandsons of the William Zeckendorf who had commandeered Webb & Knapp in the late 1940s, working in partnership with Goldman Sachs and Eyal Ofer's Global Holdings, had a vision for a grand apartment building that Robert A. M. Stern and his office carried out. The first step was to reexamine the site's zoning, as a result of which it was determined that two separate buildings—one park-side, following the Central Park West street wall, and another taller building behind it on Broadway—would be the best use of the site.[1] With that model established, Stern and the Zeckendorfs made the bold—and expensive—decision to clad the façades of the

OPPOSITE The swooping roofline and giant arch at the top of the building is a salute to the roofline of Candela's 1040 Fifth Avenue.

281

The MAYFLOWER
15 CENTRAL PARK WEST

ABOVE LEFT Designed by Emery Roth, the Mayflower Hotel consisted of two buildings, each with a distinctive water tower, that were joined through the lobby in about 1928.

ABOVE RIGHT By the early 2000s, the respectable and comfortable building and the vacant lot behind it presented a tremendous development opportunity.

OPPOSITE Floor plan. An apartment on an upper floor of the tower features views in all four directions. A thirty-four-foot-long gallery connects the public rooms, including a library with a bay window.

buildings in Indiana limestone, very much a departure from the glass-curtain-wall approach that had proved so wildly popular at Perry Street. Harking back to the best buildings across the park, this measure sought to ensure that the new development would have that element of prestige and impenetrability that has defined such buildings as 834 Fifth and 740 Park for more than seventy years. In their design, Stern and his team drew elements from a number of apartment houses they admired, in effect creating a modern-day rendition of the celebrated New York apartment buildings of the 1920s.

The complex has two entrances—one on Central Park West, the other on 61st Street—and between the buildings Stern designed a motor court paved in Belgian block that is evocative of River House's elegant private turnaround. Here, an entrance pavilion, its shape inspired by Sans Souci, the summer palace of Frederick the Great in Potsdam, Germany, links the front building, or "house," and the rear, or "tower," creating a central access point for all of the apartments. With its rich marble window surrounds, domed ceiling, and lantern, the elliptically shaped lobby is lush and elegant. The simple, stylized details both inside and out recall those of 740 Park, and the cascading setbacks and asymmetrical roofline of the forty-three-story Broadway tower evoke the best of Candela. The swooping roofline and giant arch to the north, as well as the bold colonnade stretching north–south across the top of the building, are in effect a salute to the roofline of Candela's 1040 Fifth Avenue, where Jacqueline Kennedy Onassis once enjoyed the penthouse apartment with its great terrace, elaborately asymmetrical screen, and colonnade. Stacked bay windows, like those at River House, emphasize the soaring verticality of the tower.

Every effort was made to re-create the ambience of the great prewar buildings. All of the more than two hundred apartments in the two buildings have high ceilings and generously proportioned public rooms. Each building has two elevator banks, creating private or semiprivate elevator landings, and all of the units, which range from one-bedroom to full-floor apartments, have multiple exposures. For the most part, both the tower and the house have four apartments per floor, but on the higher floors there are fewer, and larger, apartments. The nineteenth floor of the house, for example, boasts a 6,600-square-foot residence with a skylighted foyer, oval-shaped bedroom, and wraparound terrace on three sides.

Historically, West Side apartment buildings tended to have evocative names—the Dakota, the Beresford, the San Remo, and so forth—but this complex simply goes by its address, 15 Central Park West, yet another allusion to its counterparts across the park. Like 998 Fifth Avenue at the time of its completion, the mere mention of "15 CPW" is enough to conjure the complex in all its glory, not only in New York but all across the globe. Indeed, the success of 15 CPW has exceeded all expectations. The condominiums sold quickly, and many have since changed hands at exponentially higher prices. The complex draws tenants from near and far, from prominent New Yorkers to foreign dignitaries and investors.

15 CPW has all the cutting-edge amenities expected of such a high-caliber building: a gym, a walnut-paneled library, a computer room, meeting rooms, and a billiard room, as well as a modernist screening room designed by Theo Kalomirakis. A swimming pool, top lit through a glass-bottomed reflecting pool on the north side of the entry pavilion, fills out the space below the motor court. A restaurant, opening out onto the courtyard and fountain to the north, evokes the private dining rooms at the Dakota and 960 Fifth Avenue.

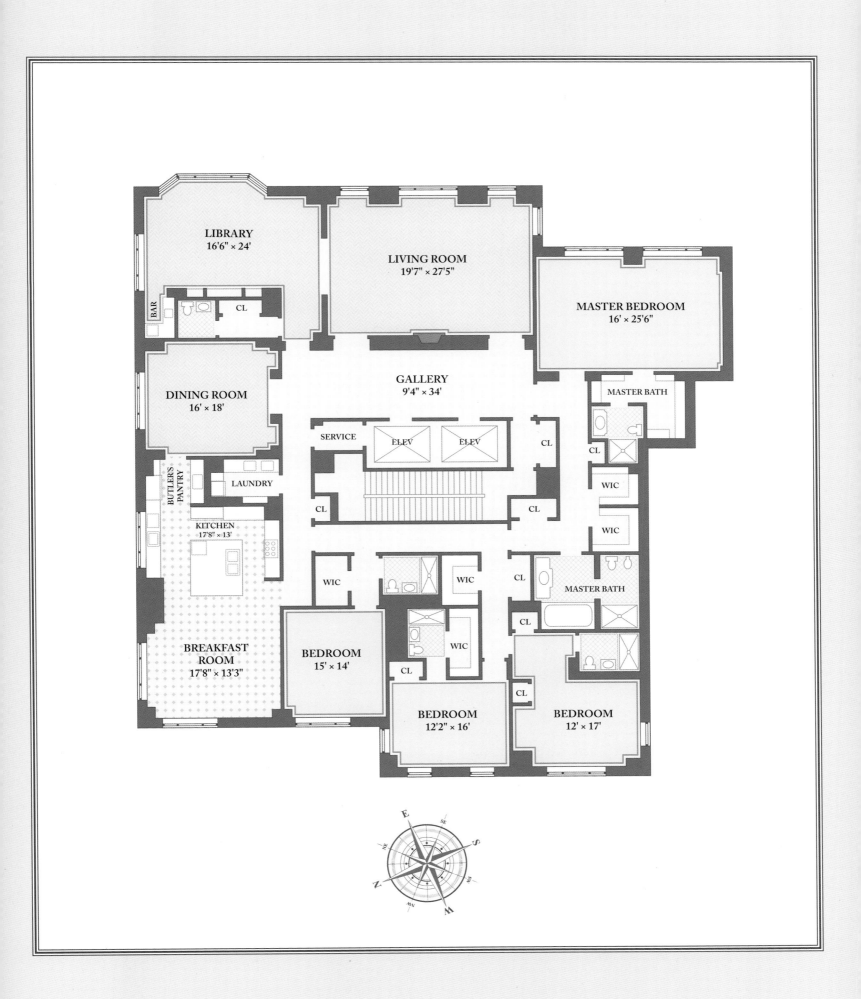

LIBRARY
16'6" × 24'

LIVING ROOM
19'7" × 27'5"

MASTER BEDROOM
16' × 25'6"

BAR

CL

MASTER BATH

DINING ROOM
16' × 18'

GALLERY
9'4" × 34'

CL

SERVICE

ELEV

ELEV

CL

CL

WIC

BUTLER'S PANTRY

LAUNDRY

CL

WIC

KITCHEN
17'8" × 13'

CL

MASTER BATH

WIC

CL

BREAKFAST
ROOM
17'8" × 13'3"

BEDROOM
15' × 14'

WIC

WIC

CL

CL

BEDROOM
12'2" × 16'

BEDROOM
12' × 17'

CL

PARK VIEW

BELOW LEFT View of the cityscape along 59th Street.

BELOW RIGHT A leaf-shaped bronze chair was designed by François-Xavier Lalanne.

OPPOSITE The views to the east stretch across the East River to Queens.

OVERLEAF In the living room, the interior design team, Nathalie and Virginie Droulers, used a palette of light green and beige, creating a calming aerie in the sky. The centerpiece is a round coffee table ringed with cushioned seating that Nathalie Droulers designed after a piece that the owners had admired at a friend's. The sofas were custom made in Italy. The painting on the easel is by Brenna Giessen.

Like many of the inhabitants of the building, the owners of this skyscraping aerie customized their apartment, asking the twin-sister team of Nathalie and Virginie Droulers, of Droulers Architecture, to carry out the interiors. The Milan-based pair injected the rooms with a distinctive geometric flair inspired by the work of Piet Mondrian. Emphasizing handcrafted finishes, they created a series of sophisticated spaces with unique elements, including inlaid bronze strips to invigorate floors and doors, and leather and lacquer paneling to define walls. Nathalie designed a number of custom furnishings that coexist comfortably with retro pieces in a mix of old and new and used a muted palette that does not compete with the amazing views to the east, north, and west. With built-ins throughout, the millwork, closets, and bathrooms have the streamlined quality of a boat in which everything has its place. The kitchen, designed to look like a study, features extensive wood paneling that conceals any appliances that might undermine the library-like ambience. Taking full advantage of the apartment's space and light, the Droulers fashioned a one-of-a-kind dwelling abounding in architectural interest and exquisite detail.

OPPOSITE The floor in the front hall is inlaid with bronze strips, as are the white-lacquered doors leading into the dining room. Paintings by Patricia Fabricant adorn the walls.

RIGHT The stylized Art Deco door in the front hall was inspired by a 1940s Milanese door. A 1950s Italian chair sits next to a table designed by Guglielmo Ulrich. The photograph is by Isabel Magowan, and the lamp is by Paul Evans.

BELOW The bronze pocket door between the front hall and the library features geometric openings. Flanking the door are posters by Charles Loupot on the left and Tato (Guglielmo Sansoni) on the right. A painting by Giacomo Ballo hangs in the library. Beyond the library is the master bedroom.

The leather and bronze panels covering the dining room walls create a Mondrian-like grid effect. An oversized chandelier by Hervé Van der Straeten hangs above the round dining table, which has a Lazy Susan built into its center. A painting by Brenna Giessen, chairs by Guglielmo Ulrich, and an antique African raffia-and-leather rug, laid over the bronze-inlaid floors, complete the décor.

OPPOSITE An intimate
breakfast area off of the kitchen
has a panoramic view of the
West Side of Manhattan and
the Hudson River through a
floor-to-ceiling window.

ABOVE Most of the appliances
in the kitchen have been hidden
behind wood panels, giving
the space the look of a library.
The stove is concealed with a
bronze cover.

LEFT The design of all of the bathrooms is different; in this one, a television is concealed behind a mirror.

RIGHT AND BELOW In one of the master bathrooms, all of the surfaces echo the elliptical shape of the ceiling; the sink, shower, bathtub niche, and even the design embedded in the frosted-glass window are curved.

OPPOSITE TOP The light fabric panels and black-lacquer framing of the master bedroom's walls give it a geometric quality. The poster over the bed is by Jean Carlu, and the chairs are by Promemoria in Milan.

OPPOSITE BOTTOM In a guest bedroom, a geometric pattern painted on one of the walls echoes the pattern of the inlaid strips of copper in the sycamore-paneled wall behind the bed. Nathalie Droulers designed the furniture in a way that concealed wires. The painting is by Brenna Giessen.

· 432 ·
PARK AVENUE

A S ONE OF THE MORE RECENT ADDITIONS TO THE MANHATTAN SKYLINE, 432 PARK
Avenue represents the new shape and direction of apartment design in the twenty-
first century. At ninety-six stories, it is the tallest residential building in the Western
Hemisphere, its spare glass form dramatically rising in one straight shot to 1,396 feet.
With deceptively simple façades, it is an engineering feat that has transformed the
city's horizon, both from the street and from the sky.

Until 2007, the Drake Hotel, a twenty-one-story Beaux-Arts building designed by Emery Roth,
occupied the northwest corner of 56th Street and Park Avenue. Developed by Bing & Bing in 1926,
the 495-room hotel fit the contours of Terminal City, the stretch of Park Avenue and its environs
between 42nd and 57th Streets. In the 1910s and 1920s, after the newly electrified railroad tracks were
buried underground in conjunction with the building of the new Grand Central Terminal, the area
was improved with a series of elegant brick and limestone apartment buildings and hotels. But as
this section of Park Avenue lost its residential appeal in the 1950s and 1960s, many of the buildings
were converted into offices and refaced with new façades and curtain walls. The Drake—once the
preferred accommodations of touring rock bands such as Led Zeppelin and The Who—remained
a stalwart within the changing neighborhood. In the 1970s, when William Zeckendorf owned the
Drake, it housed Shepheard's—named after the glamorous Shepheard's Hotel in Cairo—one of the
most fashionable nightclubs in town. Swissotel acquired the building in the 1980s and Lafayette, the
hotel's restaurant, run by Michelin-star French chef Louis Outhier and his talented young protégé
Jean-Georges Vongerichten, quickly became a culinary hotspot.

Tried-and-true New York developer Harry Macklowe, seeing promise in the Drake's location, purchased the hotel for $440 million in 2006. In 2010 co-developer CIM Group joined Macklowe, and
they commissioned Rafael Viñoly Architects to design a residential tower that would maximize the
potential for views, despite a location amid a sea of tall midtown
buildings. The Uruguayan-born architect and his team, responsible for such innovative modern designs as the Tokyo International
Forum, the circular Laguna Garzon Bridge in Uruguay, and the
walkie-talkie-shaped 20 Fenchurch Street in London, devised
a creative solution. A conventional reading of the site's zoning

OPPOSITE An expansive
window in the living room
frames views of Central Park,
the George Washington Bridge,
and points north.

ABOVE LEFT The elegant Drake Hotel, designed by Emery Roth in 1926, occupied the site of 432 Park for eighty-five years.

ABOVE RIGHT Shepheard's, named after the glamorous Shepheard's Hotel in Cairo, was a popular Egyptian-inspired nightclub at the Drake in the 1970s.

OPPOSITE Floor plan. A full-floor suite on an upper story of the building is organized around the elevator core and contains a large living room, library, dining room, eat-in kitchen, a master suite with his-and-her bathrooms, and five additional bedrooms. The apartment has unrivaled views in all four directions.

would have produced a building much like Candela's apartments of the late 1920s, but Viñoly's office used parabolic modeling software to generate a clever interpretation based on the square, the purest form of geometry. By setting the bulk in the center of the block, with only a six-story freestanding cube filling out the Park Avenue street wall and an entrance plaza on 56th Street, they made certain that the building could rise unadulterated, in accordance with zoning regulations, to unprecedented heights.

Taking his cues from the square plan, Viñoly used a grid of six ten-foot-square windows to define each façade, an approach inspired by the work of Austrian architect Josef Hoffmann and American artist Sol LeWitt. Forming the exoskeleton of the building, the grid—in addition to the elevator core's sheer walls—bears the vertical loads, freeing the interiors of columns. To break the monotony of the façades and relieve the considerable wind forces created by such a tall perpendicular structure, Viñoly separated the building into six distinct sections, in effect creating six buildings stacked one on top of another. With two-story air-gap floors reserved for mechanical systems in between the sections, Viñoly allowed for the air to pass through, reducing any unpleasant oscillations and, at the same time, creating a slightly different architectural expression to animate the façades.

Macklowe, CIM, and Viñoly dedicated the bottom portion of 432 Park, up to the twenty-ninth floor, to retail, mechanicals rooms, building offices, and the all-important amenities. Like 15 Central Park West, 432 Park was designed to compete within the international arena, and luxuries such as the indoor swimming pool, fitness center, library, screening room, conference spaces, and playroom were the expected norm. The twelfth floor is entirely occupied by the building's private restaurant and lounge, designed by Bentel & Bentel, the well-known hospitality-design firm responsible for the interiors of some of the city's most distinguished restaurants. It opens out to a private terrace overlooking 57th Street. The elegant and minimalist limestone and wood-paneled lobby is open and bright.

Soaring above are the apartments, which command sensational views; on the uppermost floors, the vista of the rivers and out to the ocean, high above the city's landmarks, is astonishing. With twelve-and-a-half-foot ceilings, the interiors of the apartments, designed by Deborah Berke Partners, are defined by the light and views. They range from two-bedroom units to a six-bedroom penthouse, and though most floors contain two apartments, some have been combined into larger full-floor suites. Responsible for the layouts, finishes, and details, Berke's minimalist design emphasizes the recessed windows, which frame the views in every room, creating smaller places within the large, column-free spaces.

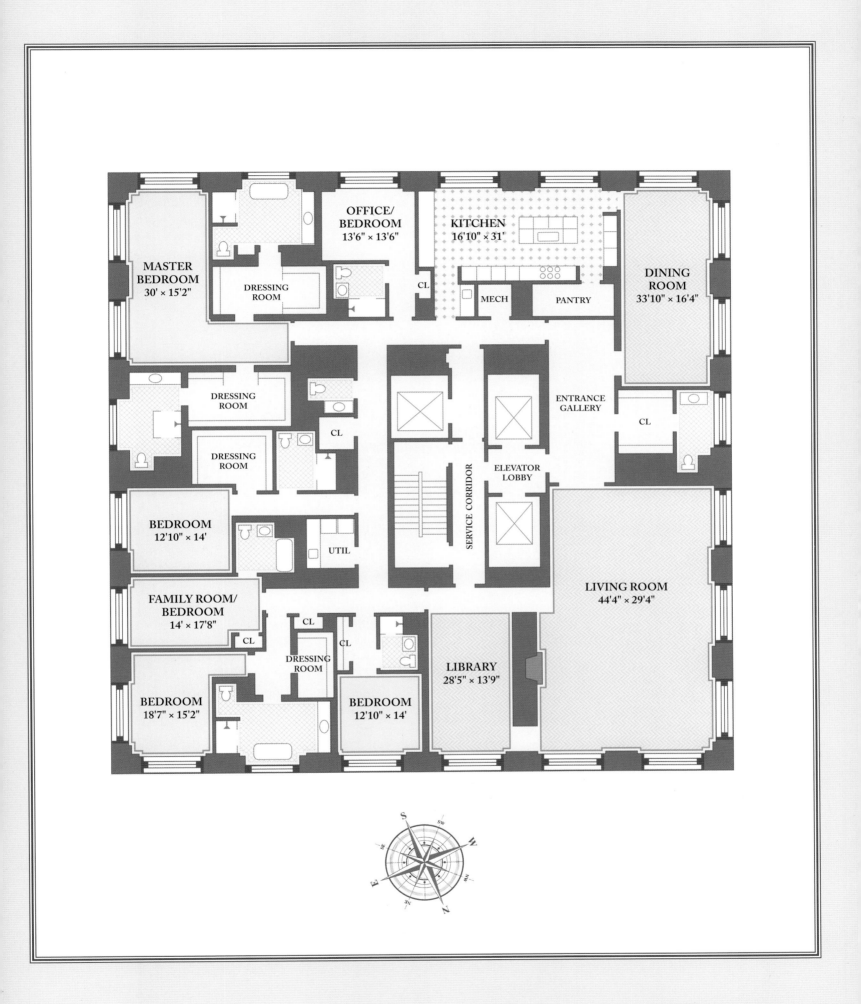

MASTER
BEDROOM
30' × 15'2"

DRESSING
ROOM

OFFICE/
BEDROOM
13'6" × 13'6"

KITCHEN
16'10" × 31'

CL

MECH

PANTRY

DINING
ROOM
33'10" × 16'4"

DRESSING
ROOM

CL

ENTRANCE
GALLERY

CL

DRESSING
ROOM

SERVICE CORRIDOR

ELEVATOR
LOBBY

BEDROOM
12'10" × 14'

UTIL

LIVING ROOM
44'4" × 29'4"

FAMILY ROOM/
BEDROOM
14' × 17'8"

CL

CL

CL

CL

DRESSING
ROOM

LIBRARY
28'5" × 13'9"

BEDROOM
18'7" × 15'2"

BEDROOM
12'10" × 14'

APARTMENT IN THE SKY

This 86th-floor apartment, decorated by Robert Couturier, is redolent of the designer's signature wit and elegance. The New York–based Couturier first found success with a major commission for Sir James Goldsmith at La Loma on the Pacific coast of Mexico and since has become recognized for his luxurious rooms both here and abroad. Though he has tempered his wonted grand style to suit the minimalism of the space, the décor nevertheless reverberates with the color and verve that characterize his work. In addition to custom-designed furnishings by Couturier's office, the rooms include a number of contemporary and vintage pieces, modern art, and colorful wall coverings and mirrors that reflect his capacity to combine different pieces in a vibrant and effortless fashion. Touches of whimsy include the Fornasetti-papered bedroom hallway and dressing room and a grouping of floral mirrors on a wall in the living room that reflect the sky high above Central Park.

At 96 stories and 1,396 feet, 432 Park is the tallest residential tower in the Western Hemisphere.

ABOVE The maroon-lacquered walls and vintage rug from Patterson Flynn Martin in the entry hall pack a powerful punch, vividly contrasting with the paler palette of the living room. Couturier covered the cushions of a custom-designed bench in a Pierre Frey fabric.

OVERLEAF A whimsical grouping of turquoise flower mirrors by Hubert le Gall embellishes the wall between two of the living room's ten-foot-square, west-facing windows. The mirrors hang over a walnut, leather, and patinated-bronze cabinet by Maarten Baas from the Carpenters Workshop Gallery and echo the color of an Eileen Grey lounge chair from Ralph Pucci International.

PRECEDING PAGES A colorful art installation by Sol LeWitt enlivens the wall behind a secondary seating area in the living room. A pair of Gio Ponti side tables flank a brown velvet Jayne sofa by Liz O'Brien. The window seat creates a quiet nook to take in the western view.

ABOVE AND OPPOSITE For the daybed that Couturier designed in the family room, which opens off of the entry hall, he created a cozy alcove adorned with a floral-patterned wall covering by Lisa Fine with a maroon felt accent wall and a "Plateau" mirror from Profiles. The curtain trim is by Holland & Sherry.

OPPOSITE The window in
the kitchen is the perfect
spot for a marble breakfast
bar overlooking northern
Manhattan and Queens.

ABOVE The kitchen, designed
by Deborah Berke Partners,
is sleek and minimalist, with
marble floors and white-
lacquered cabinetry.

LEFT Fornasetti wallpaper depicting layered arcades adds architectural interest to the bedroom hallway and dressing room.

ABOVE A freestanding tub
in the master bathroom
perches dramatically over
the Hudson River.

LEFT A Dmitry & Co. bed upholstered in a Loro Piana fabric, a bench covered in a striped Maharam fabric, and a multihued rug from Patterson Flynn Martin add splashes of color to a guest room, one of the apartment's three bedrooms.

BELOW For the custom-designed bed in the master bedroom, Couturier covered the headboard in an Oscar de la Renta fabric that coordinates with the wallcovering and custom trim on the curtains, both by Holland & Sherry.

ABOVE A beige-colored wall covering from Sonia's Place, curtains in a patterned fabric by John Robshaw, a green accent chair, and a walnut dresser from Modern Living Supplies complement the red accents in the guest bedroom.

OVERLEAF The master bedroom enjoys an unrivaled view looking south toward the Empire State Building, One World Trade Center, and the Hudson River.

ACKNOWLEDGMENTS

I wish to thank my delicious wife, Fernanda Kellogg, for her endless love, patience, and support, as she is the one who suffered though my angst.

Mark Magowan—the most erudite publisher possible. His knowledge of and enthusiasm for design and the decorative arts are inspiring.

Anne Walker—this book would not exist without her research genius and ability to express that knowledge in such elegant terms.

The Vendome Press team: Jacqueline Decter, Celia Fuller, and James Spivey, who handle editing, design, and production with extraordinary talent, ease, and good cheer. They comprise a well-oiled, efficient machine and they clearly enjoy themselves and each other.

Edward Lee Cave—the ultimate connoisseur of so many things, but especially of Manhattan's fine residential properties. He is a wonderful source of "unspoken" information and my truest mentor.

Elizabeth Stribling—an elegant lady of quality, without whose support and invaluable friendship neither this book nor my life in real estate would be the same.

Elizabeth Ann Stribling-Kivlan—a force of nature and knowledge, EA is my link to the next generation. From the book's inception, her enthusiasm and childhood memories of visiting these buildings were very helpful.

Jennifer Callahan Dickerson—my partner in business and the best sidekick ever. My life would be in shambles without her diligence, intelligence, and perennial good humor.

Others who provided important support in producing this book include: Will Zeckendorf, Christine Schwarzman, Michael Gross, Susan Nitze, Andrew Alpern, Serena Boardman, Mark Gilbertson, and Claudia Goldstein.

Kirk Henckels

I would like to begin by thanking Andrew Alpern, whose book *Apartments for the Affluent* first fueled my interest in apartment buildings and perhaps even architecture in general. I must have been no older than thirteen when I received it as a birthday present. I used to pore over its pages and try to create equally luxurious and well-designed apartments of my own, filling pad after pad of graph paper with plans of buildings. In some ways, things have come full circle—except that I do not design the apartments but write about them.

This book has been a pleasure to work on. First, thank you to my co-author, Kirk Henckels, for including me in the project. Second, I would like to acknowledge all the apartment owners who have shared their interesting and splendid homes with us, and everyone—from decorators to architects—who has helped us along the way. The photography team of Michel Arnaud, Pavel Kaminsky, and stylists Jane Creech and Katie Giustiniani has been great to work with. Celia Fuller's chic and classy book design is the perfect vehicle to showcase Michel's stunning photography. Thank you also to the team at Vendome: Jim Spivey for orchestrating the nuts and bolts of the project, Jackie Decter for her thorough and smart editing, and Mark Magowan for being the guiding light behind this book.

Anne Walker

OPPOSITE In a dining room at 998 Fifth Avenue, a pair of William Gomm chairs made in 1763 for Stoneleigh Abbey sit beneath an early eighteenth-century Chinese panel on silk paper and canvas.

NOTES

INTRODUCTION

1. "New York Apartment Houses," *The Architectural Record* 11, July 1901, 447.

THE DAKOTA

1. "The Dakota: A Description of One of the Most Perfect Apartment Houses in the World," *Daily Graphic,* September 10, 1884, reprinted in the *New York Times,* October 22, 1884, 5.
2. Ibid.
3. Edward Clark at a meeting of the West End Association in 1879, as quoted in Andrew Alpern, *The Dakota: A History of the World's Best-Known Apartment Building* (New York: Princeton Architectural Press, 2015): 170.

998 FIFTH AVENUE

1. "The Multiple Residence," *Architecture and Building* 44, March 1912, 100.
2. "New York Has the World's Costliest Apartment," *New York Times,* December 7, 1913, SM8.
3. Ibid.

820 FIFTH AVENUE

1. The Growth of Clubs in New York City," *Real Estate Record and Builder's Guide* 45, March 8, 1890, 6.
2. "A New York Fifth Avenue Apartment Building," *The Architectural Review* 5, October 1917, 225–26; pls. 59–63.

ONE SUTTON PLACE SOUTH

1. "To Put Apartment Next to Sutton Place," *New York Times,* January 10, 1925, 9.

960 FIFTH AVENUE

1. "Lawyer Buys Duplex in New 5th Av. House," *New York Times,* February 24, 1929, 162.
2. "Last Word," *The New Yorker,* September 15, 1928, 19.

720 PARK AVENUE

1. 730 Park was developed by the Northview Investing Corp., headed by Alfred Selisberg. Selisberg was also head of the Montelenox Corp., which built 720 Park. The building was designed by Lafayette A. Goldstone.
2. Kenneth Hollister Straus, *Reflections* (privately published), 7. This book was published posthumously and edited by Joan Adler of the Straus Historical Society, Smithtown, New York.

3. "New Park Av. Flat to Cost $6,000,000," *New York Times,* March 3, 1928, 32.
4. T-Square, "The Sky Line: Setbacks with Garnishings—Two to a Block—Mid-City Tower," *The New Yorker* 51, July 20, 1929, 67.

THE BERESFORD

1. "West Side Homes Facing the Park," *New York Times,* November 25, 1928, RE2.
2. Ibid.
3. "New Rental Record Made on West Side," *New York Times,* September 15, 1929, RE1.
4. Ibid.

10 GRACIE SQUARE

1. "Apartments Ready for Fall Rental," *New York Times,* September 8, 1929, RE1.
2. "Artistic Tower Effects," *New York Times,* November 23, 1930, 156.

740 PARK AVENUE

1. T-Square, "The Skyline: St. Bartholomew's Dome— The Sun and the Spire—Park Avenue Pair," *The New Yorker,* June 21, 1930, 68.
2. As quoted in Michael Gross, *740 Park: The Story of the World's Richest Apartment Building* (New York: Broadway Books, 2005): 291.

778 PARK AVENUE

1. T-Square, "Skyline," *The New Yorker,* as quoted in Christopher Gray, "Streetscapes: Fraternal-Twin Examples of East Side Superluxury," *New York Times,* June 8, 2003, RE5.
2. "New Era For Park Av.," *New York Times,* April 26, 1931, RE1.

RIVER HOUSE

1. "Huge River Apartment," *New York Times,* October 13, 1929, RE2.
2. Augusta Owen Patterson, "The East River as a Major Motif," *Town & Country,* September 1, 1932, 40.
3. "River Club Interests Society," *New York Times,* May 4, 1930, XII.
4. River Club's interiors are described in Augusta Owen Patterson, "An Exercise Club in a Romantic Setting," *Town & Country,* February 1, 1931.

15 CENTRAL PARK WEST

1. Rafael Pelli had originally designed a scheme for Avlon that consisted of two buildings on a podium. Peter Claman of SLCE Architects reexamined the zoning to come up with a more compelling alternative, the basis of Stern's design.

BIBLIOGRAPHY

Alpern, Andrew. *New York's Fabulous Luxury Apartments*. New York: Dover Publications, 1987.

———. *The New York Apartment Houses of Rosario Candela and James Carpenter*. New York: Acanthus Press, 2002.

———. *The Dakota: A History of the World's Best-Known Apartment Building*. New York: Princeton Architectural Press, 2015.

Frazer, Susan Hume. *The Architecture of William Lawrence Bottomley*. New York: Acanthus Press, 2007.

Gross, Michael. *740 Park: The Story of the World's Richest Apartment Building*. New York: Broadway Books, 2006.

———. *House of Outrageous Fortune: Fifteen Central Park West, the World's Most Powerful Address*. New York: Atria Books, 2014.

Pennoyer, Peter, and Anne Walker. *New York Transformed: The Architecture of Cross & Cross*. New York: The Monacelli Press, 2014.

Ruttenbaum, Steven. *Mansions in the Clouds: The Skyscraper Palazzi of Emery Roth*. New York: Balsam Press, 1986.

Sexton, R. W. *American Apartment Houses, Hotels and Apartment Hotels of Today*. New York: Architectural Book Publishing Co., 1929.

Stern, Robert A. M., Gregory Gilmartin, and Thomas Mellins. *New York 1930: Architecture and Urbanism Between the Two World Wars*. New York: Rizzoli, 1988.

PHOTO CREDITS

All photographs by Michel Arnaud, with the exception of the following:

Page 15: (left) Peter Arno/The New Yorker Collection/The Cartoon Bank, © Condé Nast. **Page 18:** (top) Photographer unknown/Museum of the City of New York. X2010.11.1587; (bottom) Jack Robinson/Archive Photos/Getty Images. **Page 19:** (top) Brian Hamill/Premium Archive/Getty Images; (bottom) Henry Groskinsky/The LIFE Images Collection/Getty Images. **Page 20:** Horst P. Horst/Condé Nast Collection/Getty Images. **Page 38:** (top) Irving Underhill (1872–1960)/Museum of the City of New York. X2010.28.178; (bottom left) Entrance Hallway, 998 Fifth Avenue, photograph; from the McKim Mead & White Architectural Records Collection (PR42), box 46, folder: Century Holding Co., image #93802d, New-York Historical Society; (bottom right) Exterior with automobile, 998 Fifth Avenue, photograph; from the McKim Mead & White Architectural Records Collection (PR42), box 46, folder: Century Holding Co.; photo by Robt W Tebbs, image #93801d, New-York Historical Society. **Page 39:** (top) Samuel H. (Samuel Herman) Gottscho (1875–1971)/Museum of the City of New York. 88.1.1.4236 and 88.1.1.3938; (bottom) Apt. Reception Room, 998 Fifth Avenue, photograph; from the McKim Mead & White Architectural Records Collection (PR42), box 46, folder: Century Holding Co., image #93803d, New-York Historical Society. **Page 66:** Courtesy of Piet Boon BV. **Page 69:** (bottom) Cecil Beaton/Condé Nast Collection/Getty Images. **Page 70:** Photographs © John Hall. **Pages 72–81:** Courtesy of Piet Boon BV. **Page 84:** (left) Wurts Bros. (New York, N.Y.)/Museum of the City of New York. X2010.7.1.3267; (right) Wurts Bros. (New York, N.Y.)/Museum of the City of New York. X2010.7.1.3269. **Page 85:** (left) Cecil Beaton/Condé Nast Collection/Getty Images. **Page 102:** (left) Samuel H. (Samuel Herman) Gottscho (1875–1971)/Museum of the City of New York. 88.1.1.644; (right) Wurts Bros. (New York, N.Y.)/Museum of the City of New York. X2010.7.2.21088. **Page 118:** (top left) Wurts Bros. (New York, N.Y.)/Museum of the City of New York. X2010.7.2.7492; (top right) McNeir apartment interior, 720 Park Avenue; from the Mattie E. Hewitt & Richard A. Smith Photograph Collection (PR26), box 14, folder 337, image #93804d, New-York Historical Society; (bottom) Samuel H. (Samuel Herman) Gottscho (1875–1971)/Museum of the City of New York. 88.1.1.1046 and 88.1.1.1302. **Page 119:** Courtesy of the Straus Historical Society, Inc. **Page 148:** (top left) Wurts Bros. (New York, N.Y.)/Museum of the City of New York. X2010.7.2.15616; (top right) George P. Hall and Son/Museum of the City of New York. 92.53.89; (bottom) Samuel H. (Samuel Herman) Gottscho (1875–1971)/Museum of the City of New York. 88.1.1.1460. **Page 149:** (left) Susan Wood/Archive Photos/Getty Images; (right) Todd Plitt/Contour by Getty Images/Getty Images. **Page 168:** (top) Samuel H. (Samuel Herman) Gottscho (1875–1971)/Museum of the City of New York. 88.1.1.1852; (bottom) Samuel H. (Samuel Herman) Gottscho (1875–1971)/Museum of the City of New York. 88.1.1.2635 and 88.1.1.4236. **Page 169:** (top left) Samuel H. (Samuel Herman) Gottscho (1875–1971)/Museum of the City of New York. 88.1.1.1859; (bottom left) Edward Steichen/Condé Nast Collection/Getty Images; (right) Horst P. Horst/Condé Nast Collection/Getty Images. **Page 184:** Courtesy of Rockefeller Archive Center. **Page 185:** (left) Slim Aarons/Masters/Getty Images; (top right) Unidentified maker, *Electra Havemeyer Webb at the 740 Park Avenue apartment*, ca. 1925. Gelatin silver print, 7 x 5 in. Collection of Shelburne Museum Archives. PS3.2-194; (bottom right) Unidentified maker, *Interior of 740 Park Avenue apartment*, date unknown. Gelatin silver print, 10 x 8 in. Collection of Shelburne Museum Archives. PS3.15-33. **Page 209:** (top left) Estate of Evelyn Hofer/Masters/Getty Images; (bottom) Photograph © Billy Cunningham. **Pages 212–13:** Photograph © Marco Ricca. **Page 226:** Samuel H. (Samuel Herman) Gottscho (1875–1971)/Museum of the City of New York. 88.1.1.2083, 88.1.1.2058, 88.1.1.2101, and 88.1.1.2134. **Page 242:** (top) Wurts Bros. (New York, N.Y.)/Museum of the City of New York. X2010.7.1.7084; (bottom) Samuel H. (Samuel Herman) Gottscho (1875–1971)/Museum of the City of New York. 88.1.1.2820. **Page 243:** Samuel H. (Samuel Herman) Gottscho (1875–1971)/Museum of the City of New York. 88.1.1.2040, 88.1.1.2031, 88.1.1.2077, and 88.1.1.2038. **Page 264:** (bottom) Photograph © Francesco Tonelli. **Page 282:** (left) Wurts Bros. (New York, N.Y.)/Museum of the City of New York. X2010.7.2.3029. **Page 298:** (left) Wurts Bros. (New York, N.Y.)/Museum of the City of New York. X2010.7.1.8460; (right) Slim Aarons/Premium Archive/Getty Images. **Page 300:** Photograph © DBOX.

Best efforts were made to verify all photo credits. Any oversight was unintentional and should be brought to the publisher's attention so that it can be corrected in a future printing.

ENDPAPERS Detail of Nancy
Lorenz's incised, water-gilt,
and burnished yellow gold-leaf
panels in the powder room of
an apartment at One Sutton
Place South.

PAGE 1 Carved detail in an
apartment at 998 Fifth Avenue.

PAGES 2–3 Piotr Uklański's
Untitled (The Hole), 2007, bathes
an original curved stair and
balustrade at 740 Park Avenue
in red light. The front hall in
the apartment also showcases
Joe Bradley's *Zoroaster*, 2009,
and, under the stair, Nate
Lowman's *White Escalade*,
2005–8.

PAGES 4–5 The traditional
character of a living room
at 720 Park Avenue has been
revitalized with red pocket
doors, a mix of contemporary
and vintage furnishings,
and vibrant art, including
a *Rorschach* painting by
Vik Muniz.

PAGES 6–7 A black-and-white-
themed living room at 10 Gracie
Square features an eclectic mix
of art and objects, including
works by Lee Bul, Richard
Artschwager, Rachel Feinstein,
Rob Wynne, David Shrigley,
and Tom Sachs.

PAGES 8–9 LEFT A library
decorated by Bunny Williams
at 740 Park Avenue retains its
original paneling. RIGHT An
intricately carved mantel in a
library at 740 Park Avenue.

PAGES 10–11 The spectacular
view of the park from the
terrace of a penthouse at
15 Central Park West.

ABOVE From a window
at 834 Fifth Avenue, the
distinctive silhouette of
15 Central Park West can
be seen across the park.

First published in the United States of America by

THE VENDOME PRESS

www.vendomepress.com
Vendome is a registered trademark of The Vendome Press, LLC

ISBN 978-0-86565-340-5

EDITOR: Jacqueline Decter
PRODUCTION DIRECTOR: Jim Spivey
PRODUCTION COLOR MANAGER: Dana Cole
DESIGNER: Celia Fuller
APARTMENT PLANS: Claudia Goldstein

Library of Congress Cataloging-in-Publication Data

Names: Henckels, Kirk, author. | Walker, Anne, 1973- author. | Arnaud,
  Michel, photographer (expression)
Title: Life at the top : New York's most exceptional apartment buildings /
  Kirk Henckels, Anne Walker ; photography by Michel Arnaud.
Description: New York : Vendome Press, 2017.
Identifiers: LCCN 2017025864 | ISBN 9780865653405 (hardback)
Subjects: LCSH: Apartment houses--New York (State)--New York--History. |
  Manhattan (New York, N.Y.)--Buildings, structures, etc. | New York
  (N.Y.)--Buildings, structures, etc. | BISAC: ARCHITECTURE / Buildings /
  Residential. | ARCHITECTURE / Interior Design / General. | DESIGN /
  Interior Decorating.
Classification: LCC NA7862.N5 H46 2017 | DDC 728/.31409747--dc23
LC record available at https://lccn.loc.gov/2017025864

This book was produced using acid-free paper, processed chlorine free,
and printed with soy-based inks.

Printed in China by OGI
SECOND PRINTING